HYPER-
ACTIVI-
TYPO-
GRAPHY

FROM A TO Z

gestalten

HELLO
BOYS AND GIRLS!

Welcome to

HYPERACTIVITYPOGRAPHY FROM A TO Z

As y'all know, typography is FUN. And kinda superawesome, too!

But ... Becoming a real-deal-hyperactivitypographer takes quite a bit! You actually have to eat, drink and breathe typography. Yes, you have to be truly familiar with rather common terms like: Alphabet, alternate character, ampersand, apex, arabic number, arc of the stem, arm, ascender, autoflow, banner, bar, baseline, bastard, beak, Bezier curve, bleed, body copy, body size, boldface, bold type, book list, bounce, boustrophedon, bowl, bracketed serif, brackets, break, bullet, caching, calendaring, calligraphy, cap height, cap line, capital, caption, centered, character, character set, codex, cold type, column rule, condensed, connotation, contrast, counter, cross bar, cross stroke, crotch, cuneiform, cursive, cutline, denotation, descender, diacritic, dingbats, discretionary hyphens, display face, downloadable font, drop cap, ear, Egyptian, em, em dash, em square, em space, em unit, embedding, expanded, extended, fixed pitch, flex, font, font family, font style, Fontographer, foot, footer, Gothic, geometric, glyph, greeked text, gutter, hanging indent, head, header, headline, hyperactivitypography, hyphenation zone, I-beam, ideograph, indents, initial cap, inline graphic, insertion point, italic, jumplines, justified, kerning, kicker, leader, leading, legibility, left justified, letter spacing, ligature, line spacing, logotype, lowercase, majuscules, margins, mean line, metrics, monospaced font, multiple master font, oblique, Old Style, OpenType, orphan line, outline font, overprinting, paragraph, permanent font, petroglyph, pica, pictograph, pitch, pixel, point, point size, PostScript, printer font, proportionally spaced type, proportional spacing, pull quotes, ragged, rasterization, readability, recto, rendering, resident font, resonance, reverse type, right justified, Roman, running footer, running header, sans serif, scalable font, screen font, script, serif, set-width, semiautomatic flow text, sidebars, side bearing, slant, slug, soft font, small caps, spacing, spread, spur, square serif, standoff, stem, stress, stretched text, style, style sheet, subhead, substrate, swash, tab, tab marker, tab stop, tail, teaser, terminals, text block, text face, text wrap, thin space, threaded text blocks, track kerning, tracking, transient font, transitional, TrueType, type, Type 1 PostScript font, Type 3 PostScript font, typeface, typestyle, type size, Uncial, uppercase, verso, vertex, weight, widow line, word spacing, word wrap, x-height, x-line... Stuff like that.

However, if some of these words don't ring a bell
then we can only advice you to become seriously interhyperactive with

HYPERACTIVITYPOGRAPHY FROM A TO Z

By the way:
Do you know how many different typefaces have been used in this foreword?
And how many font sizes (both picas AND points)? And how many true and faux italics?
And how many ligatures? Do you know?!

Either way enjoy!

BEFORE YOU START

Some things you should do before you get hyperactive with this book:

1. GET YOUR SUPPLIES IN ORDER.

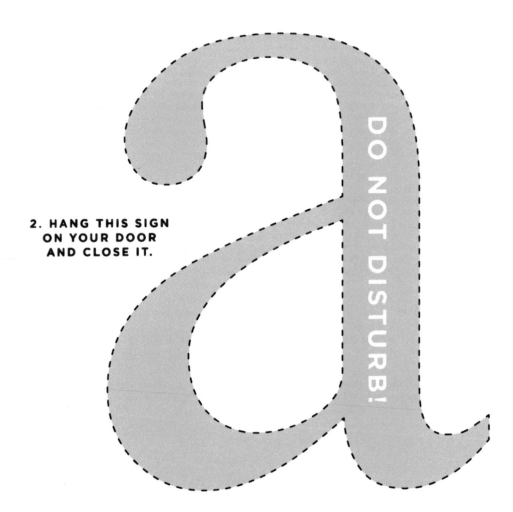

2. HANG THIS SIGN ON YOUR DOOR AND CLOSE IT.

DO NOT DISTURB!

3. MAKE A CUP OF TEA OR COFFEE.

4. PUT ON YOUR FAVOURITE WORK TUNES.

5. SET YOUR MIND ON TYPE.

You'll find extra sheets in the back on which you can practice your skills!

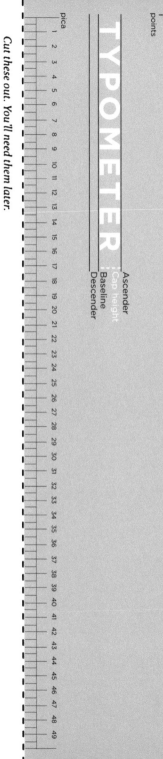

Cut these out. You'll need them later.

TYPOMETER

pica

1 2 3 4 5 6 7 8 9 10 11 12 13 14 15 16 17 18 19 20 21 22 23 24 25 26 27 28 29 30 31 32 33 34 35 36 37 38 39 40 41 42 43 44 45 46 47 48 49

Ascender
Cap height
Baseline
Descender

points

4 5 6 7 8 9 10 11 12 13 14 15 16 17 18 19 20 21 22 23 24 25 26 27 28 29 30 31 32 33 34 35 36 37 38 39

LINE SPACING

4 5 6 7 8 9 10 11 12 13 14 15

16 17 18 19 20 21

A

IS FOR

AMPERSAND

*What other words with an A
can YOU think of?*

A typographical term:

....

A typeface:

....

COPY RIGHT

A1 • *Practise on these lettershapes by copying the form again and again and again.*

A A A A A A

B B B B

C C C

Math + typography = true

A2

$V + V =$ $\mathcal{W}$

$W \cdot 180° =$

$A + (O \cdot 0,1) =$

$0^2 =$

Cool!

LIKE FATHER like son

A3 • *Can you help the fathers find their sons?*

FATHER	son
FATHER	son
FATHER	son
FATHER	son
FATHER	**son**

Where's the head, shoulder, leg and foot, leg and foot?

TRUE OR FAUX

Yeah right!

A5 • *Can you tell the difference between a true italic and a faux one?*

1. Italic
T ☐ F ☐

1. Italic
T ☐ F ☐

2. Italic
T ☐ F ☐

2. Italic
T ☐ F ☐

3. Italic
T ☐ F ☐

3. Italic
T ☐ F ☐

4. Italic
T ☐ F ☐

4. Italic
T ☐ F ☐

Which typeface is it?

1. ....
2. ....
3. ....
4. *Arno*

A6 •
Find five typographical errors.

Arial

Just Kidding

What does a typographer, a claustrophobic and an astronaut have in common? They're all occupied with space.

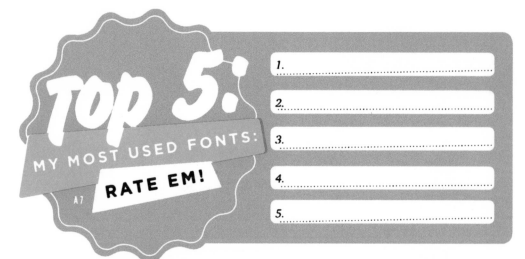

TOP 5:

MY MOST USED FONTS:

RATE EM!

A7

1. ....
2. ....
3. ....
4. ....
5. ....

WHERE'S (ш)ALDO?

A8 • *Aldo is a futuristic typeface who is stuck in typographic past! Help us find him and bring him back to the future!*

QUICK FOX VS LAZY DOG

A9 • *Can you find the words that describe the image?*

```
S  N  E  B  S  X  Q
M  W  U  E  P  O  U
I  O  T  X  M  F  I
L  R  H  B  U  A  C
I  B  E  Z  J  Z  K
```

```
D  R  E  V  O  R  M
O  J  E  H  T  L  W
G  D  P  P  A  K  J
L  F  L  Z  Z  D  U
X  R  Y  T  V  H  P
```

CRAZY COMBINATIONS

It's wacky!

A10 • *This is total chaos. Which typefaces are combined here?*

A
1. ....
2. ....

B
1. *Stencil*
2. ....

X
1. ....
2. ....

DRAW THE LINE!

Manage this!

A12 • *Are you worthy of the 'typographer' title?*
Test your knowledge on this question.

WHO WANTS TO BE A
TYPOGRAPHER
WHO WANTS TO BE A

When did type founding and typeface design begin?

A *Mid-15th century*

B *Early 16th century*

C *Late 17th century*

D *Mid-18th century*

B

IS FOR

BLACKLETTER

*What other words with a B
can YOU think of?*

A typographical term:

....

A typeface:

....

2 is a pair!

B1 • *Find the typeface to match the image.*

A ☐ MATCH ME!   C ☐ Match me!   E ☐ MATCH ME!

B ☐ **Match me!**   D ☐ **Match me!**   F ☐ Match me!

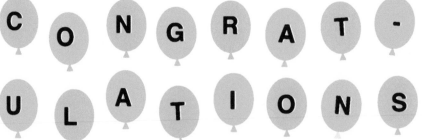

CONGRAT- ULATIONS

B2 • *This typeface celebrated its 50th anniversary in 2007.*

What is the name of the font?
....

Who designed it?
....

In which country was it born?
....

CIRCULAR
CAUSE & EFFECT

B3 • *Which came first?*

Ink

OR

Pen

Smile

OR

Smiley

B4 • *Rorschach tests are often used to see what state of mind a patient is in. Which letter(s) do you see and how do you feel about that?*

NEVILLE BRODY

Homage

TO A
TYPE DESIGNER

B5 • *Pay a tribute to the designer above. It can be inspired by his personality, his typefaces or something entirely different. Be playful!*

Respect!

TYPE
FACE

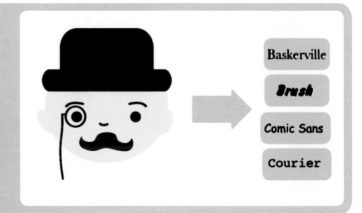

Baskerville

Brush

Comic Sans

Courier

B6 • *Match the face with a typeface!*

B7 • *Which typeface is the word below written in? Don't believe the type!*

TIMES

IS IT WRITTEN IN ...
A) *Times Bold?*
B) *Adobe Jenson Bold?*
C) *Bookman Old Style Extra bold?*

DON'T LOSE FACE!

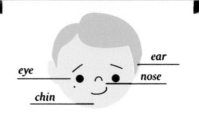

ear

eye

nose

chin

B8 • *Which is not a typographical term?*

MATCHMAKER! **B9** • *Can you find the matching pairs?*

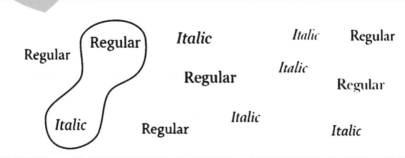

Regular

Regular

Italic

Italic

Regular

Italic

Italic

Regular

Italic

Regular

Regular

Regular

Italic

WANNA-B'S:

B10 • *Can you sort out who's for real?*

B vs. B   B vs. B   B vs. B

B11

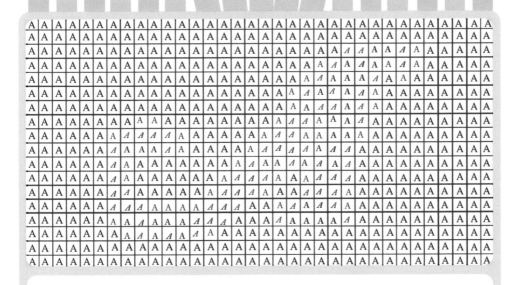

COLOUR BY FONT

Adobe Caslon Pro Regular

Adobe Caslon Pro Italic

Adobe Caslon Pro Semibold

Adobe Caslon Pro Semibold Italic

Adobe Caslon Pro Bold

Adobe Caslon Pro Bold Italic

THREEE ON A ROW

B12 • *Play with a friend. Only perfect O's and X's are approved.*

X	O	
O	X	X
O		X

TO B OR NOT TO B...

B13 • *Which typeface is Hamlet holding in his hand? (Clue: It starts with a B.)*

THE FONT IS: ....

B14 CREATE A *Typographical* TATTOO

Just Kidding

What's megalomania? A typographer who thinks the universe isn't spaced properly.

C

IS FOR

CALLIGRAPHY

*What other words with a C
can YOU think of?*

A typographical term:

....

A typeface:

....

Make your own LIGATURE

C1 • *Make a ligature using the letters: F and X!*

Five Senses — SIGHT

C2 • *Which typeface looks best on this particular kind of paper?*

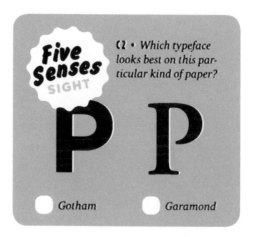

P ⬭ Gotham

P ⬭ Garamond

> **What's in a name?**

C3 • *What's in a font's name? How does the name reflect the font? Make up a name for the font used in the quote above.*

NAME: ....

GLYPHORAMA **C4 •** *Circle the bogus glyph!*

ə Ħ Á Ų ǵ Þ ß

Ş ğ Ŀ ± ¢ Đ ō

'ALL TYPEFACES ARE EQUAL, BUT SOME TYPE-FACES ARE MORE EQUAL THAN OTHERS.'

▲ **C5 •** *All the words are written in sans-serif typefaces. But can you find the word written in the least equal typeface? And can you guess which typeface it is?*

C6

FIND FIVE TYPOGRAPHICAL ERRORS

CUT IT OUT!

*(7 • This is your new mantra! Cut it out and hang it over your desk.
It will bring good luck for years to come!*

SPOT IT!

C8 • *Spot the matching shadow:*

Rub it in!

C9 • *Make a rubbing of embossed typography you fancy:*

Swash me up!

C10 • *Draw swashes on these handsome letterforms. Don't be afraid to go over the top with this one!*

Juicy!

Transformers

C11 • *Turn these sans-serif letters into beautiful seriffed ones –*
it can be done! Simply draw serifs on the existing letterforms.

abcde

TQ

C12 • *Test your Typographical Quotient*
(TQ) and figure out how well you know
letters and typography. What is the
missing figure?

Example

Test

Alternatives

D

IS FOR

DINGBATS

What other words with a D
can YOU think of?

A typographical term:

....

A typeface:

....

MAKE A T

D1 • *Help the poor boy by dressing him up in the coolest T you know.*

Alright!

Cap line

Mean line

Baseline

TYPOMETER

D2 • *Fill in the typefaces you love and loathe at the moment.*

AWESOME!

D3 • *Find the typographer's mouse.*

HOT

NOT

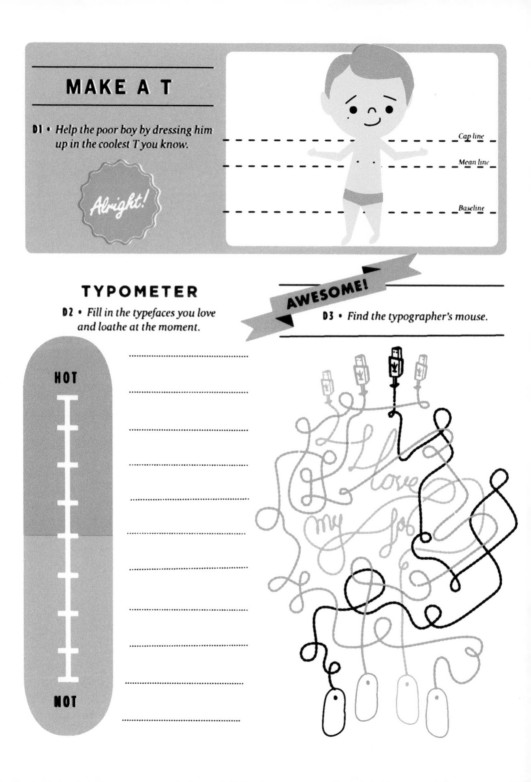

Ampersand study

D4 • *Can you find a font for each ampersand listed below? Can you also find two ampersands of your own? Draw them in the last empty frames.*

| 1 | 2 | 3 | 4 | 5 | 6 | 7 | 8 | 9 |

1: Garamond Italic

2: ....

3: ....

4: ....

5: ....

6: ....

7: ....

8: ....

9: ....

FAMOUS FIRST ▶ WORDS

D5 • *What do you think these typefaces would say if they could speak? Write down their first words:*

Comic Sans

Adobe Garamond Pro

D6.1 • How large is the spacing between the shelves? (Use the typometer. You'll find it in the front of this book.)
Your measurement: .... pt.

D6.2 • How many letters are in the jar on the counter?

☐ 19 ☐ 18 ☐ 21

D6.3 • Can you recognize the typefaces decorated on the cookies on the counter?

1 ....

2 ....

3 ....

4 ....

D6.4 • The shop keeper needs help from a trained hand to draw some cool typography on some boxes of alphabet candy. Can you help him?

D6.5 • There is a major typeface sale going on! And best of all: Some of them are free! Can you tell which ones are for free and which aren't? Match the prices below with the correct typefaces by writing them on the posters.

FREE $35 $29

D6.6 • Who has written the book displayed in the books section?

D6.7 • Are you cool or a fool when it comes to buying typefaces? Test your attitude on these statements:
A) When I've bought a typeface, everyone can use it.
True ☐ False ☐

B) As long as I only use one letter from a typeface, it's free.
True ☐ False ☐

C) It's considered a real crime if I use a typeface I'm not licensed to use.
True ☐ False ☐

100% OFF! SALE! **FREE FONTS!** OVER HERE!

D6.8 • Which of these characteristics are common for free fonts?

☐ **Bad kerning**

☐ Strange Letterforms

☐ ░░░ ░░░░░░░░░

GOOD PLACES TO BUY TYPEFACES:

www.myfonts.com
www.fontshop.com
www.linotype.com
www.adobe.com/type

A–Z

WHAT'S ON THE TYPOGRAPHER'S MIND?

D7 • *Can you see the answer?*

Manage this!

GREATER OR LESSER THAN

D8 • *Which of the typefaces below has the greatest number of weights?*
Put > , < or = between the typefaces to suggest which is greater, lesser and equal.

Caslon		Garamond
Myriad		Helvetica
Bickham		*Zapfino*
Times		Times New Roman
Futura		Avant Garde

WHAT HAVE I DONE?

– Adrian Frutiger

D9 • *Rearrange the words to get the answer.*

1. MUNAKULHER ➝ ....
2. NEIDYPTENE ➝ ....
3. SRENIVU ➝ ....
4. COR-B ➝ ....
5. NASTURACI ➝ ....

Just Kidding

Which jumpy little creature is a typographer by nature?
Kern-it the frog.

E

IS FOR

EGYPTIENNE

*What other words with an E
can YOU think of?*

A typographical term:

....

A typeface:

....

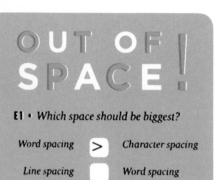

OUT OF SPACE!

E1 • *Which space should be biggest?*

Word spacing	>	Character spacing
Line spacing	☐	Word spacing
Character spacing	☐	Line spacing

Just Kidding

What makes a poor typographer?
Lack of character.

E2

LET'S FIND THE TYPO-GRAPHER

What type am I?

E3 • *Play the game 'Guess Who' with fonts instead of celebrities!*

  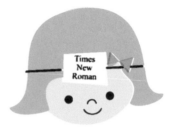

Possible questions:
– Am I bold?

– Do I have big eyes?
– Am I condensed?

– Are my ears large?
– Am I italic?

TYPEFACE IT!

E4 • *Draw a face by only using these 10 glyphs:*

ôõ••}~*(OU

"Cool!"

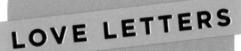
LOVE LETTERS

E5 • *How well do these typefaces get along? Is it love in the air or just a fling?*

A + A = ...1%.....

A + A = ...

A + A = ...

A + A = ...

E6 • *Practise your calligraffiti on the train.*

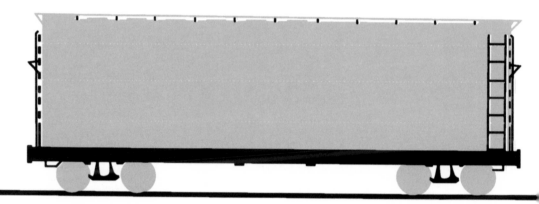

HIDDEN
CHARACTER

E7 • *How well do you know Mr. Baskerville?*

B, E OR F?

Show skills!

Surname

E8 • *Name the typedesigner and his typeface:*

Francois ....
John ....
Claude ....
William ....
Giambattista ....

WHO'S CALLING?

E9 • *Look at the numbers on the telephone and guess right.*

....

E10 •
Find five typographical errors.

Helvet ica

P   P

Who doesn't belong?

P   P

WHICH BELONG TOGETHER?

E12 • *Find the ones that belong together!*

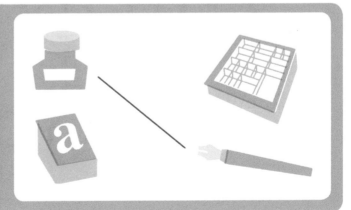

NEVERMORE

E13 • *Can you find the letters with a beak in the word above? Circle the letters.*

E14

Find the hidden ambigram

LETTERFORM ANATOMY

E15 • *Figure out the typographic terms and fill inn the right answers.*

It's complicated!

HtiQfgxR

aeTyp fi

F

IS FOR

FLEURONS

*What other words with an F
can YOU think of?*

A typographical term:

....

A typeface:

....

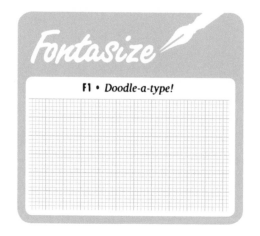

Fontasize

F1 • *Doodle-a-type!*

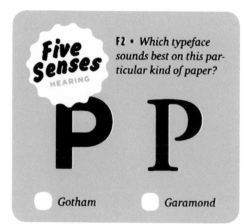

Five Senses
HEARING

F2 • *Which typeface sounds best on this particular kind of paper?*

P P

○ Gotham   ○ Garamond

inish decorating the drop cap. Finish decorating the drop cap. Finish decorating the drop cap. Finish decorating the drop cap. Finish decorating the drop cap. Finish decorating the drop cap. Finish decorating the drop cap. Finish decorating the drop cap. Finish decorating the drop cap. Finish decorating the drop cap. Finish decorating F3

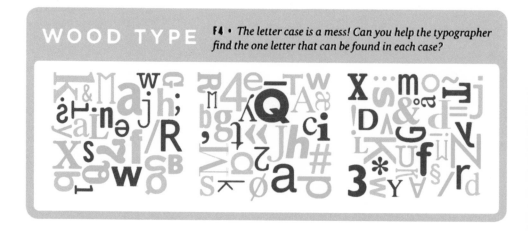

WOOD TYPE

F4 • *The letter case is a mess! Can you help the typographer find the one letter that can be found in each case?*

WHAT TYPE IS IT?

F5 • *Numbers alone won't do the job. Typefaces are what a true typographer is more interested in! Can you tell what typefaces the numbers are set in?*

Tahoma

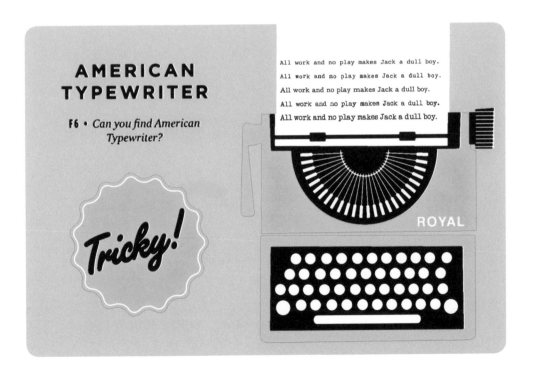

AMERICAN TYPEWRITER

F6 • *Can you find American Typewriter?*

Tricky!

All work and no play makes Jack a dull boy.
All work and no play makes Jack a dull boy.
All work and no play makes Jack a dull boy.
All work and no play makes Jack a dull boy.
All work and no play makes Jack a dull boy.

ROYAL

SHOOT!

F1 • Circle the places where the letters overshoot the line. Can you also draw in a couple of more letters that overshoot?

ABCabc

TYPOGRAPHIC TIMELINE

F8 • Match the typographic phenomenon to the right year.

LATIN ALPHABET

ERIC GILL

MOVEABLE TYPE

PAPER

GUTENBERG

THE BOOK

MR. GARAMOND

ITALIC

4000   3000   700   0   1450   1455   1490   1501   1882

1	2	3	4	5	6	7	8	9
I	*2*							

When do you use old style numbers?

Lower case ⬭   Small caps ⬭   Uppercase ⬭

Says who?

Which designer said all this: 1. 'To me designing has never been a job or profession. It's a way of life, like a priest or rabbi.' 2. 'I don't think that success is the premise to what is good or bad.' 3. 'The contributions that one makes in typography, design, and art in general cannot be, and must not be measured on how much money is involved. That would lead to total chaos. The word itself (contribution) is to give to a common purpose.'

F10
....

ADRIAN FRUTIGER

OPEN TYPE

MS. TWOMBLY

INDESIGN

1928 1959 1983 1992 1996 1999 2002 2008 2010

TRUE OR FAUX

Yeah right!

F11 • *Can you tell the difference between a true bold and a faux one?*

1. Bold	1. Bold
T ○ F ○	T ○ F ○
2. Bold	**2. Bold**
T ○ F ○	T ○ F ○
3. Bold	3. Bold
T ○ F ○	T ○ F ○
4. Bold	**4. Bold**
T ○ F ○	T ○ F ○

Which typeface is it?

1. ....
2. ....
3. *Caslon*
4. ....

OPEN TYPE

F12 • *What does the inside of the letters look like?*

F13 • *Are you worthy of the 'typographer' title? Test your knowledge on this question.*

WHO WANTS TO BE A TYPOGRAPHER

What was the name of the first typeface used to print books in Europe?

A *Garamond*

B *Gutenberg*

C *Caslon*

D *D-K Type*

G

IS FOR

GROTESQUE

*What other words with a G
can YOU think of?*

A typographical term:

....

A typeface:

....

G is for GLASSES

GILL   JOHNSTON

61 • *Draw the correct glasses on the font designers:*

Math
+ typography
= true

a+e= ....

N · 90º= ....

(=)+L= ....

C+Ɔ= ....

MOVIE MADNESS

63 • *Can you recognize these movie titles? Figure out which movie it is and finish the film titles.*

Do it, dude!

LOST & FOUND(RY)

64 • *Various characters have been piling up lately and it's time to tidy up! The characters have been categorized in different boxes. Now, can you write the name of the rightful owner on the boxes, so they'll find their way home safely?*

Property of:
....

Property of:
....

Property of:
....

Property of:
Font Font

Property of:
....

Property of:
....

Exclusive!

CHOOSE FROM THE FOLLOWING RIGHTFUL OWNERS:

Emigre	Hoefler & Frere J.	Font Bureau	Font Font	House Ind.

Just Kidding

Who's an expert in type-faeces?
A typoographer.

ROMAN NUMERALS

65 • *Translate the roman numerals.*

I		II	
V		IV	
X		IX	
L		LVI	
C	100	XXI	
D		MXIVC	
M		MCMXCIX	

66 • Which G do you find most beautiful? Circle your favorite or draw your own!

G G G G
G

Says who?

'Anyone who would letterspace black letter would steal sheep.'

67 •
....

TYPEFACE PROFESSION

5 The Fashion Designer

The Carpenter

The Barber

The Disc Jockey

The Painter

68 • Which typeface and profession are best suited for each other?

1. EUROSTILE   **2. ROSEWOOD**   3. COPPERPLATE   *4. Brush Script*   5. DIDOT

69 • *Try to pixelate this beautiful serif lettershape by using the grid to the right. Try capturing as many details as possible. You can do it!*

Don't be square!

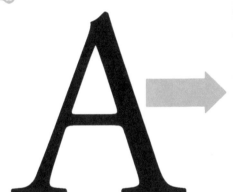

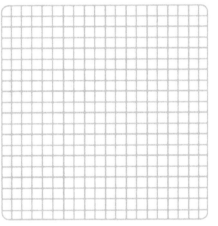

GUESS THE NON-TYPOGRAPHICAL TERM!

G10 • *Can you guess which of the images below doesn't show a typographical term?*

Figure it out!

A

B

C

WHICH FONT WOULD BE THE BETTER LISTENER?

g g **g** g g

g g **g** g **g**

g g g g g

Be all ears!

611 • *Find the G with the biggest ear and circle it! Can you also tell which typeface it is?*

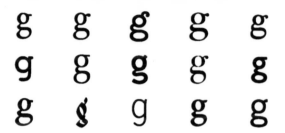

GILLICIOUS!

612 • *Which of the items below does <u>not</u> originally use Gill Sans? Cross out the wrong ones.*

PENGUIN BOOK

BOOK **BOOK TITLE** BOOK
AUTHOR NAME

BBC

iMac

UNDERGROUND

TOMMY

HILFIGER

UNITED COLORS OF BENETTON.

LUCKY STRIKE

Subway
Brooklyn
Atlanic Av Station

B D M N R
1 2 3 4 5

CHANEL

H

IS FOR

HAMBURGEFONS

What other words with an H
can YOU think of?

A typographical term:

```
.................................
```

A typeface:

```
.................................
```

MATCHMAKER!

M1 • *Can you find the matching pairs?*

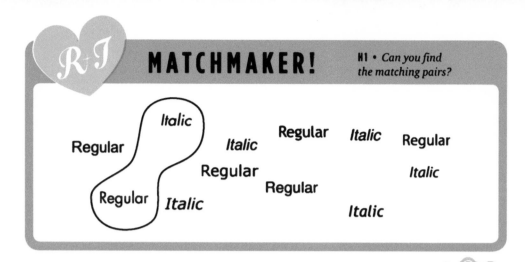

BAREFOOTED SHOPPING SPREE

Stylish!

M2 • *Misses Minion is spending her husband's income on new shoes and she needs something that brings out the best in her. Help her choose the best matching shoes from the shelf below!*

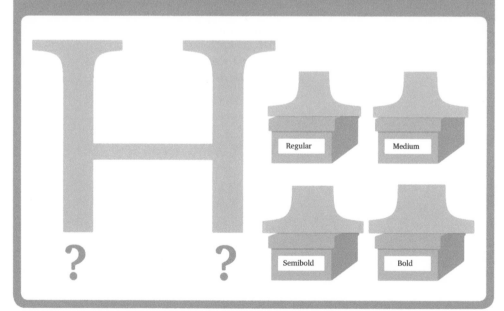

H4 • *Doodle-a-type!*

H3 • ....

SHOW THE HIDDEN CHARACTERS

H5 • *10 font names of both new and classic typefaces are hidden below. Can you find them?*

H	X	R	E	T	R	A	H	C	N	I	D	U
L	H	E	R	C	U	L	A	N	U	M	W	U
A	A	V	E	N	E	G	M	A	H	T	O	G
R	E	N	O	D	N	E	R	A	L	C	T	J
N	G	L	N	A	I	D	R	A	W	D	E	D
O	X	E	P	A	P	T	A	R	U	K	K	A

H6 • *Oh no! The font has been pixelated! It's now up to your patience and design skills to restore the cleanliness of the font. Draw the outline on the lettershapes and place vector points in the ideal places to secure the best looking letter shapes. May the pen tool be with you!*

ABCDEFGH

abcdefgh

Edgy!

MAKE YOUR OWN POP-UP!

H7 • *Just cut along the dotted lines and fold where the solid lines are. Once you pop, you can't stop!*

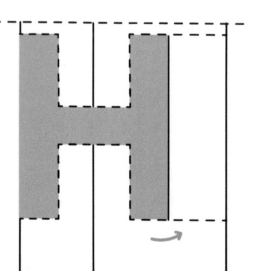

LIKE FATHER like son

H8 • *Can you help the fathers find their sons?*

FATHER	son
FATHER	son
FATHER	son
FATHER	son
FATHER	son

Which
TYPEFACE
are you?

THIS ONE? *THIS ONE?* *THIS ONE?* *THIS ONE?*

H9 • *Which typeface do you share personality traits with? Take the test to find out!*

1. WHICH WORDS BEST DESCRIBE YOU?
A) *Normal, a bit boring, reliable.*
B) *Traditional, snob, classic.*
C) *Intellectual, tortured soul, artistic.*
D) *Easy-going, funny, premature.*
E) *Geeky, weird, crazy.*

2. WHAT ARE YOU DOING ON A FRIDAY NIGHT?
A) *Pizza and a movie.*
B) *Tea party with my rich friends.*
C) *Working on an art project.*
D) *Doing pranks.*
E) *LAN-party.*

3. WHAT KIND OF MUSIC DO YOU LIKE?
A) *Rock.*
B) *Classical.*
C) *Soul.*
D) *Pop.*
E) *Techno.*

4. WHAT ARE YOUR FAVOURITE COLOURS?
A) *I have no preferance.*
B) *Pale, cool nuances.*
C) *Black, gray, white.*
D) *Rainbow colours.*
E) *RGB.*

5. WHO DO YOU BELIEVE IN?
A) *Myself.*
B) *God.*
C) *Nothing.*
D) *Satan, but just out of spite.*
E) *Aliens.*

6. WHAT'S YOUR FAVOURITE GADGET?
A) *iPhone.*
B) *Blackberry.*
C) *Notebook.*
D) *Gameboy.*
E) *Calculator.*

7. WHAT'S YOUR FAVOURITE APPLICATION?
A) *Photoshop.*
B) *InDesign.*
C) *I prefer to work by hand.*
D) *Flash.*
E) *Dreamweaver.*

8. WHAT DO YOU PREFER TO READ?
A) *Blogs.*
B) *Glossy magazines.*
C) *Books.*
D) *Cartoons.*
E) *Web coding.*

9. WHAT MOVIE GENRE DO YOU LIKE?

A) Drama.
B) Romantic.
C) Film noir.
D) Comedy.
E) Documentary.

10. WHAT'S YOUR FAVOURITE DRINK?

A) Beer.
B) Champagne.
C) Red wine.
D) Juice.
E) Soda.

11. WHAT'S YOUR FAVOURITE MODE OF TRANSPORTATION?

A) Car.
B) Limousine.
C) Walking.
D) Bicycle.
E) Public transportation.

12. IF YOU WERE TO HAVE A PET, WHAT WOULD IT BE?

A) Dog.
B) Pony or horse.
C) Cat.
D) My mom says I can't have one.
E) Guinea pig.

13. WHAT'S YOUR FAVOURITE DESIGN/ART/STYLE ERA?

A) Bauhaus, Swiss design.
B) Art nouveau, rococo.
C) Arts & crafts.
D) Pop art, new wave.
E) Web 2.0, futurism.

14. WHAT IS YOUR MANNER OF SPEAKING?

A) Normal.
B) Eloquent.
C) Don't talk much.
D) Lots of slang.
E) Not understandable.

15. WHAT DO YOU LIKE TO DISCUSS WITH FRIENDS/CO-WORKERS?

A) Randomness.
B) Money, fashion.
C) Philosophy, psychology, ideas, books.
D) Cartoons, television series, jokes.
E) Technology, coding, science.

16. WHAT'S YOUR FAVOURITE PLACE TO WORK?

A) School/workplace.
B) Home office.
C) Café.
D) Friend's house.
E) Basement.

Now, count the letters from your answers. The letter you have the most of will reveal which typeface you are.

Finished counting? Now, go to the Answers-section to find the results!

Revealing!

I

IS FOR

INSCRIPTIONAL

*What other words with an I
can YOU think of?*

A typographical term:

....

A typeface:

....

TYPOGRAPHERS PUZZLE

11 • *Which font is the typographer known for? Write the name of the font in the correct column in the right font.*

1. Francois Didot
2. Eric Gill
3. Carol Twombly
4. Claude Garamond
5. Giambattista Bodoni
6. Herman Zapf

²GILL

WHAT IS THE TYPO-GRAPHICAL TERM?

12 • ....

HIDDEN
CHARACTER

13 • *How well do you know Mr. Baskerville?*

L, D OR I?

Show skills!

I I I

Fontasize

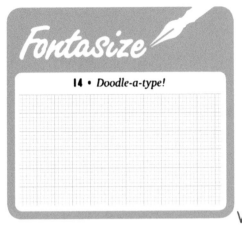

14 • Doodle-a-type!

THE MISSING EQUIPMENT

15 • *Our friend the typographer is worried. He has misplaced his typography equipment somewhere in his office! Help him find the missing items.*

THE MISSING ITEMS:

Check it out!

TYPE FACE

16 • *Match the face with a typeface!*

Futura

Brush

Times

TRAJAN

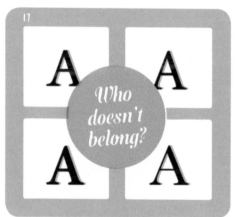

Who doesn't belong?

A   A

A   A

Make your own
LIGATURE

18 • *Make a ligature using the letters: W and H!*

WHO'S CALLING?

19 • *Look at the numbers on the telephone and guess right.*

....

CONNECT THE BULLETS I

1. Find a pencil!
2. Connect the dots A1 to A2 and so forth.
3. Read the text.

This one's easy!

A2 A1
A3 C1 C2 C3
B1
C5 C4
A4 D2
B2 E2 F1 G1 G2
D1 G3
G5 G4
E1
D3
F2

C6

CONNECT THE BULLETS II

1. Find two pencils!
2. Use tape to connect the pencils!
3. Hold them in 45 degree angle.

This one's harder!

A1 A2
D1 D2
E1 E2
B2 B3
B1 B4
C1 C2
C3
C6
A3 C4 D3
C5 D4
A4 B5 C5

111 • Which designer is celebrating?

Eric Gill   Robert Slimbach   Matthew Carter   Edward Johnston

WHAT'S THAT?!

112 • Which one's (a) an upper case I, (b) a lower case L, or (c) a number 1?

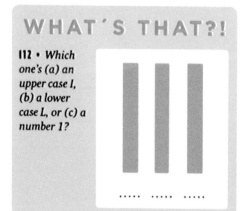

Just Kidding

Why do typographers often hang out in courtrooms? Because they like to see words getting justified.

FONTSPOTTER

113 • Are you sitting in the car, bus or train and are you kind of bored? Play a game of FONTSPOTTING and guess the fonts that are used on signs along the way!

Get out of here!

J

IS FOR

JUSTIFICATION

*What other words with a J
can YOU think of?*

A typographical term:

. . . .

A typeface:

. . . .

CHECK THIS OUT!

J1 • *Find a magnifying glass and zoom in to reveal the secret message!*

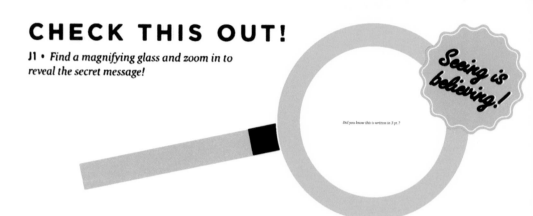

Did you know this is written in 3 pt.?

Seeing is believing!

Typeseeing

J2 • *Can you tell what these five calligraphic and typographic styles are and where they can be seen?*

1.

2.

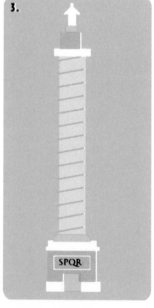

3.

SPQR

4.

5.

A ☐ Roman square capitals on the Trajan Column in Rome, Italy.

B ☐ Insular script in the Lindisfarne Gospels in London, United Kingdom.

C ☐ Runic inscription on Vimose comb in Copenhagen, Denmark.

D ☐ Rustic capitals in Vergilus Romanus in Vatican City.

E ☐ Textura script in the Gutenberg bible in Mainz, Germany.

CHEER-LEADING

Bring it on!

TEAM GILL SANS

TEAM UNIVERS

TEAM ARIAL

J3 • *The higher x-height, the higher leading. What font team requires the tallest cheer-leading members?*

....

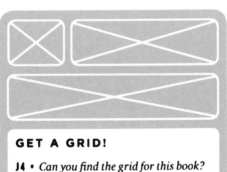

GET A GRID!

J4 • *Can you find the grid for this book? Choose a random page and draw it in (this page might be a good one).*

wtf?
WHAT THE FONT?

J5 • *Which font is the fontname below set in? Hint: Don't believe the type!*

MYRIAD

IS IT WRITTEN IN ...
A) *Myriad Semibold?*
B) *Scala Sans Bold?*
C) *Frutiger Regular?*

Font- A B C

Try to name a font for each letter in the alphabet. Bonus points: Draw the name of the font similar to how the font actually looks!

A
....

B
....

C
....

D
....

E
....

F
....

G
....

H
....

I
....

J
....

K
....

L
....

M
....

N
....

O
....

P
....

Q
....

R
....

S
....

T
....

U
....

V
....

W
....

X
....

Y
....

Z
....

Æ
....

Ø
....

Å
....

Are you having trouble naming all the letters? Why not use the opportunity to discover a new font! Here are some links to fontshops you can check out:

www.fontshop.com
www.myfonts.com
www.adobe.com/type

CAN YOU FIND TRAJAN?

J7

CONNECT THE MOLES

J8 • *And find out which typographer this is:*

_ILLIAM CASLON

OPTIC ILLUSION

J9 • *The typographer just saw an awe-ful font combination. How does he feel? You can see the answer below.*

FACELIFT

J10 • From their date of orgin, most typefaces have had a few facelifts over the years. Can you guess which typeface has had the most re-cuts?

1. Caslon
····················

2. Garamond
····················

3. Times
····················

4. Helvetica
····················

5. Akzidenz Grotesk
····················

FIND THE TYPOGRAPHICAL TERMS!

J11 • 21 typographical terms are hidden in the image below. Can you find them?

It's possible!

K

IS FOR

KERNING

*What other words with a K
can YOU think of?*

A typographical term:

....

A typeface:

....

Cut it out!

K1 • *Write your initials by cutting out the shapes and fold them.*

∧∧∧∧∧∧∧∧∧∧∧∧∧∧∧∧∧∧∧∧
∧∧∧∧∧∧∧∧∧∧∧∧∧∧∧∧∧∧∧∧
∧∧∧∧∧∧∧∧∧∧∧∧∧∧∧∧∧∧∧∧
∧∧∧∧∧∧∧∧∧∧∧∧∧∧∧∧∧∧∧∧
∧∧∧∧∧∧∧∧∧∧∧∧∧∧∧∧∧∧∧∧
∧∧∧∧∧∧∧∧∧∧∧∧∧∧∧∧∧∧∧∧
∧∧∧∧∧∧∧∧∧∧∧∧∧∧∧∧∧∧∧∧
∧∧∧∧∧∧∧∧∧∧∧∧∧∧∧∧∧∧∧∧
∧∧∧∧∧∧∧∧∧∧∧∧∧∧∧∧∧∧∧∧
∧∧∧∧∧∧∧∧∧∧∧∧∧∧∧∧∧∧∧∧

FAMOUS FIRST WORDS

K2 • *What do you think these typefaces would say if they could speak? Write down their first words:*

Say what?!

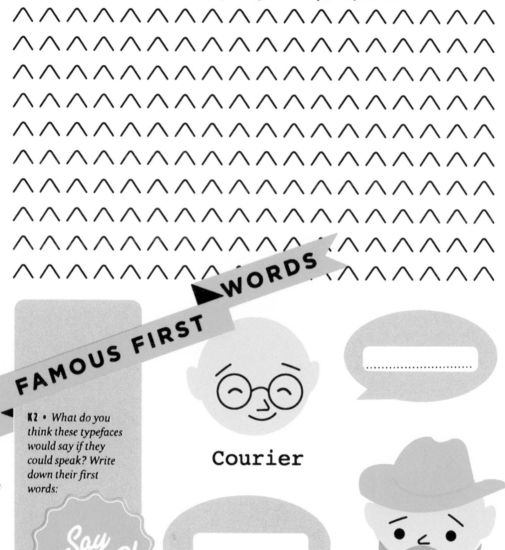

Courier

ROSEWOOD

WHICH TYPEFACE WOULD YOU BRING TO A
DESERTED ISLAND?

SANS SERIFFE

ANSWER:

K3 · ....

Things to do on Sans Seriffe:

1. Build an amper-
   sand castle.

2. Catch a B.

3. Practise
   your italic.

4. Send a letter.

5. Swim in the C.

6. Wear a cap.

7. Loose some
   weight.

« DRAW THE LETTER STROKE!

DRAW THE LINE!

K5 • *Finish the letter with your pen.*
It will improve your typographical skills!

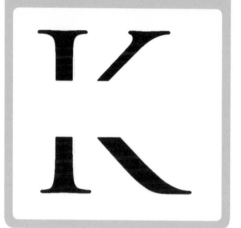

K6 • *Rorschach tests are*
often used to see what state of mind a
patient is in. Which letter(s) do you see
and how do you feel about that?

K7 • FIND 3 MISTAKES

Alright!

FONT CLASS

This is plain!

K8 • *Suggest what fonts belong in the different classes.*

ECONOMY CLASS

Narrow and condensed fonts, lower cases, economic fonts

....

....

....

....

EMERGENCY EXIT

Fonts with extra tall x-height, long acenders, extra long legs

....

....

....

....

BUISNESS CLASS

Uppercases. Capitals. Superscripts.

....

....

....

....

REAL OR FAUX?

K9 • *Amy has discovered that the purse she bought in Italy is a rip-off. Which purse is the faux italic?*

ROLL THE DICE

....

....

....

....

....

....

Impress your friends!!

L

IS FOR

LIGATURE

What other words with an L can YOU think of?

A typographical term:

....

A typeface:

....

UPPERCASE VS. CAPITALS

Yeah right!

L1 • *Can you tell the difference between uppercase and capitals?*

1. TYPE
U ☐ C ☐

1. TYPE
U ☐ C ☐

2. TYPE
U ☐ C ☐

2. TYPE
U ☐ C ☐

3. TYPE
U ☐ C ☐

3. TYPE
U ☐ C ☐

4. TYPE
U ☐ C ☐

4. TYPE
U ☐ C ☐

Which typeface is it?

1. ....

2. *Myriad*

3. ....

4. ....

Fontasize

L2 • *Doodle-a-type!*

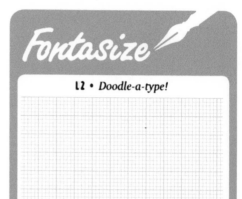

Just Kidding

A typographer is suffering from a sore throat. He's kind of worried and visits a doctor. The doctor says: 'Open your mouth and say "A".' The typographer replies: 'Can you be more specific?'

L3 • *Are you worthy of the 'typographer' title? Test your knowledge on this question.*

WHO WANTS TO BE A TYPOGRAPHER

Who's Roman typeface influenced most of the Western typefaces that followed?

A *Ludovico Arrighi*

B *Nicolas Jenson*

C *Robert Granjon*

D *Claude Garamond*

Ornament match

L 4 • *Match the ornament to the right font:*

Baskerville

Adobe Jenson Pro

Adobe Caslon Pro

Arno Pro

Brioso Pro

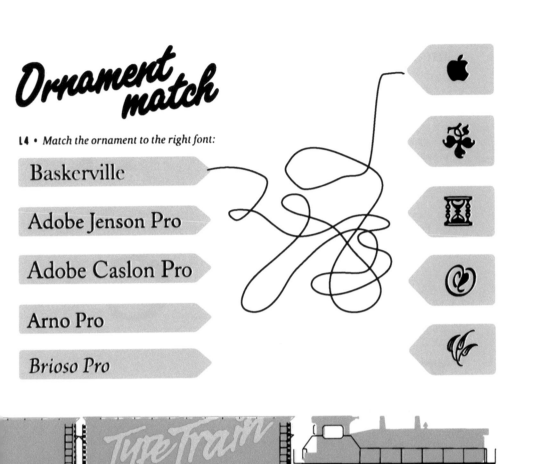

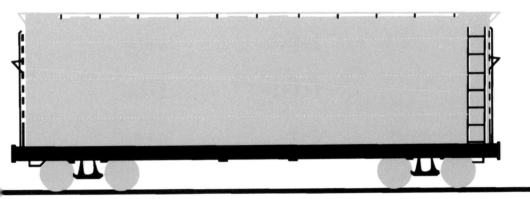

L 5 • *Practise your calligraffiti on the train.*

MEET THE

Family!

L6 • *Oh no, the family portrait wall is missing one portrait! Can you draw the fourth member of the family? Can you also guess the name of the font family?*

Family name:

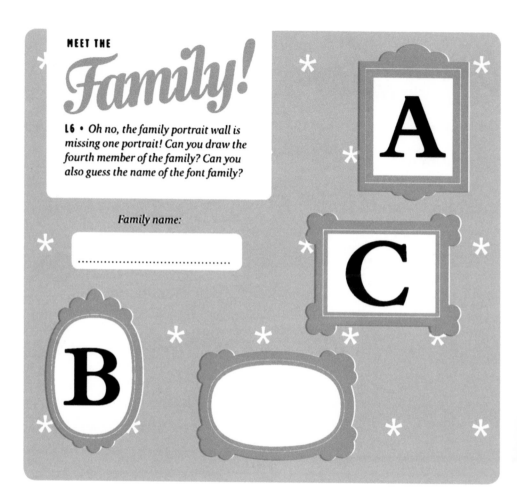

LIGATURE
Math

L7 • *Now you have the ultimate chance to show your fellow typo geeks how to merge letters like a pro!*

f+f= ....   s+t= ....

f+f+i= ....   f+i= ....

c+t= ....   a+e= ....

TYPOLITICS

★ ★ ★ ★ ★ ★ ★ ★ ★ ★ ★ ★ ★ ★ ★ ★ ★ ★

L8 • *The election is finally here and it's time to pick sides! So which party do you belong to? Cross off the party issues you agree with and find out who you should be voting for. What are ya waiting for?*

THE LIBERALS	THE CONSERVATIVES
Magazine & web	Books
Modern	Historic
Experimental	Conservative
Titles	Body text
Everyday	Festive
Helvetica	Times
Futura	Garamond
Myriad	Trajan
SUM	**SUM**

Now, count the votes! Who won?
Write a good slogan for your winning party:

★ ★ ★ ★ ★ ★ ★ ★ ★ ★ ★ ★ ★ ★ ★ ★ ★

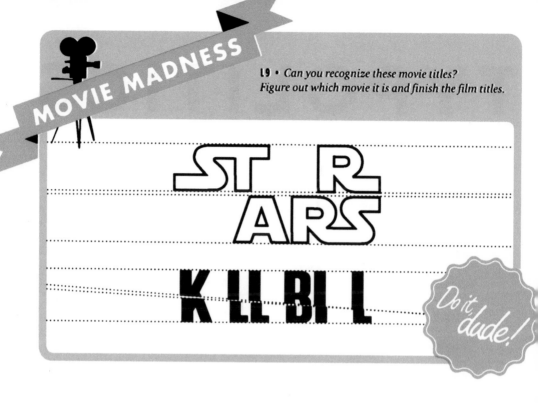

MOVIE MADNESS

L9 • *Can you recognize these movie titles?*
Figure out which movie it is and finish the film titles.

ST R
AR S

K LL BI L

Do it, dude!

LAYOUT MEETS ERA

L10 • *Which layout matches which era?*
1. renaissance 2. modernism 3. bauhaus 4. baroque

M

IS FOR

MAJUSCLES

*What other words with an M
can YOU think of?*

A typographical term:

....

A typeface:

....

DRAW THE LINE!

M1 • *Finish the letter with your pen. It will improve your typographical skills!*

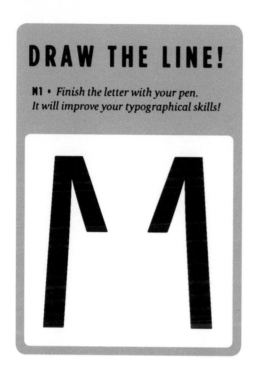

LIKE FATHER like son

M2 • *Can you help the fathers find their sons?*

FATHER   son
FATHER   son
FATHER   son
FATHER   son
FATHER   son

MOUSTACCENTS

moustache circumflex

moustache accent acute

moustache tilde

moustache accent grave

moustache tréma

M3 • *Draw the correct accents in the faces above.*

Lorem Ipsum

N4.1 • Which Lorem Ipsum is correct?

. . . . 1 . . . .
'Lorem ipsum dolor sit amet, consectetur adipisicing elit, sed do eiusmod tempor incididunt ut labore et dolore magna aliqua. Excepteur sint occaecat cupidatat non proident, sunt in culpa qui officia deserunt mollit anim id est laborum.'

. . . . 2 . . . .
'Lorem ipsum dolor sit amet, consectetur adipisicing elit, sed do eiusmod tempor incididunt ut labore et dolore magna aliqua. Duis aute irure dolor in reprehenderit in voluptate velit esse cillum dolore eu fugiat nulla pariatur.'

. . . . 3 . . . .
'Lorem ipsum dolor sit amet, consectetur adipisicing elit, sed do eiusmod tempor incididunt ut labore et dolore magna aliqua. Ut enim ad minim veniam, quis nostrud exercitation ullamco laboris nisi ut aliquip ex ea commodo consequat.'

'Neque porro quisquam est qui dolorem ipsum quia dolor sit amet, consectetur, adipisci velit ...'

N4.2 • Locate and circle the typographical term in the quote above. (You'll find a translation of the quote in the Answers section.)

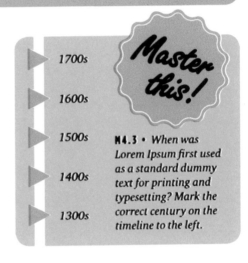

1700s

1600s

Master this!

1500s

N4.3 • When was Lorem Ipsum first used as a standard dummy text for printing and typesetting? Mark the correct century on the timeline to the left.

1400s

1300s

N4.4 • Are you worthy of the 'typographer' title? Test your knowledge on this question.

WHO WANTS TO BE A TYPOGRAPHER
WHO WANTS TO BE A

The Latin text Lorem Ipsum is based on originates from an old literary work. Which?

A Illiad by Homer

B Epic of Gilgamesh (Unknown author)

C On the Ends of Good and Evil by Cicero

D The Divine Comedy by Dante

(M)EMORY

Cut it out!!

M5 • *Lay the cards with the typeface down. Flip two and two cards to try to find the pair of font. If they do not match, the cards are turned back over and it's your friend's turn.*

M	M	M	M
M	M	M	M
M	M	M	M
M	M	M	M

INITIAL DRAWING

M6 • *Use the square to draw the first letter of your name as typographically perfect as you possibly can!*

INK SUCKERS!

M7 • *Which of these typefaces sucks the most ink?*

- [ ] Comic Sans
- [ ] Garamond
- [ ] Helvetica
- [ ] Times
- [ ] *Brush Script*
- [ ] **Impact**

M8

How to grow a letter

Get real!

-SEED

1.
2.
3.
4.
5.
6.

M9 • *A tribute to the wonderful æ.*

M9.1 • *Which countries have 'æ' in their alphabet?*

....

M9.2 • *Which English words can be written with an 'æ'?*

....

M9.3 • *What is the command for 'æ'?*

◯ Option + a   ◯ Option + d

◯ Option + o   ◯ Option + i

◯ Shift + Option + i

M9.4 • *Which letters does 'Æ' consist of?*

.... & ....

M9.5 • *Which letters does 'æ' consist of?*

.... & ....

Æ is for æmbitious …

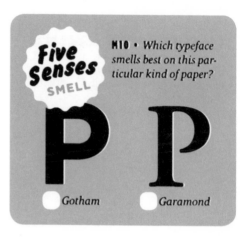

Five Senses **SMELL**

M10 • *Which typeface smells best on this particular kind of paper?*

◯ Gotham   ◯ Garamond

TRUE OR FAUX

Yeah right.

M11 • *Can you tell the difference between true & faux sub and superscript?*

Sub_1 T ☐ F ☐ Sub_1 T ☐ F ☐

Sub_2 T ☐ F ☐ Sub_2 T ☐ F ☐

$Super^3$ T ☐ F ☐ $Super^3$ T ☐ F ☐

Which typeface are they?

1. ....

2. ....

3. *Futura*

N

IS FOR

NUMERAL

What other words with an N can YOU think of?

A typographical term:

....

A typeface:

....

WHAT IS GARAMOND DOING?!

N1 • *Claude Garamond is being very mysterious. Connect the various A's, B's and C's in chronological order (alphabetical when fonts are from the same year) to reveal his big secret!*

Says who?

'Perfect typography is certainly the most elusive of all arts. Sculpture in stone alone comes near it in obstinacy.'

N2 •

....

Weird!

CROP TYPE

Corny!

N3 • *Friendly aliens left some messages behind. Do you know which typefaces they prefered?*

1

....

2

....

CLAUDE GARAMOND

Homage
TO A
TYPE DESIGNER

Respect!

N4 • *Pay a tribute to the designer above. It can be inspired by his personality, his fonts or something entirely different. Be playful!*

GOTHIC STYLES

N5 • *Can you see which gothic typeface belongs to which setting?*

1 The Bible

2  PUB

3

A GOTHIC   **B** Gothic   **C** GOTHIC

Arial vs. Helvetica

N6 • *Do you know the difference between Arial and Helvetica? In texts below four of the words have been changed out with the opposite font. Circle them out!*

Arial

Designed in 1982 by Robin Nicholas and Patricia Saunders for Monotype (not Microsoft), it's classified as Neo Grotesque, was originally called Sonoran San Serif, and was designed for IBM's bitmap font laser printers.

It was first supplied with Windows 3.1 (1992) and was one of the core fonts in all subsequent versions of Windows until Vista, when to all intents and purposes, it was replaced with Calibri.

Helvetica

Designed in 1957 by Max Miedinger, Helvetica's design is based on that of Akzidenz Grotesk (1896), and classified as a Grotesque / Transitional sans-serif face.

Originally it was called Neue Haas Grotesque; in 1960 it was revised and renamed Helvetica (Latin for Switzerland "Swiss").

TYPE HARD!

WHAT IS THE TYPO-GRAPHICAL TERM?

N7 • ....

CIRCULAR
CAUSE & ARGUMENT

N8 WHICH CAME FIRST?

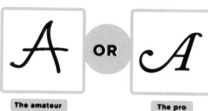

The amateur   The pro

God   Typography

Birthday cake

1

2

3

4

5

6

7

Happy birthday!

N9 · HOW TO DO IT:

1. Put some icing in the bag.
3. Close the dispenser.
4. Cut off the end.
5. Insert a paper tube in the opening to turn the dispenser into a quill.
6. Hold it in the right angle.
7. Check your spacing!

Bon appetit!

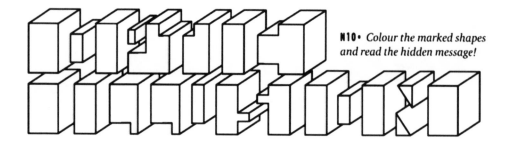

FIND THE
TYPOGRAPHICAL TERMS!

N11 • *14 typographical terms are hidden in the image below. Can you find them?*

Make a list of all the terms you find here:

....

....

IS FOR

OBLIQUE

*What other words with an O
can YOU think of?*

A typographical term:

....

A typeface:

....

Past meets present

01 • *What do the letterforms of the hieroglyphs translate to in today's letterforms?*

EGYPTIAN HIEROGLYPHS 3200 BC–400 AD	PHOENICIAN ALPHABET 1050 BC–323 BC	LATIN ALPHABET 700 BC TO THE PRESENT

N

F

A

K

H

TYPE FACE

02 • *Match the face with a typeface!*

Arial

TRAJAN

Ballpark

Courier

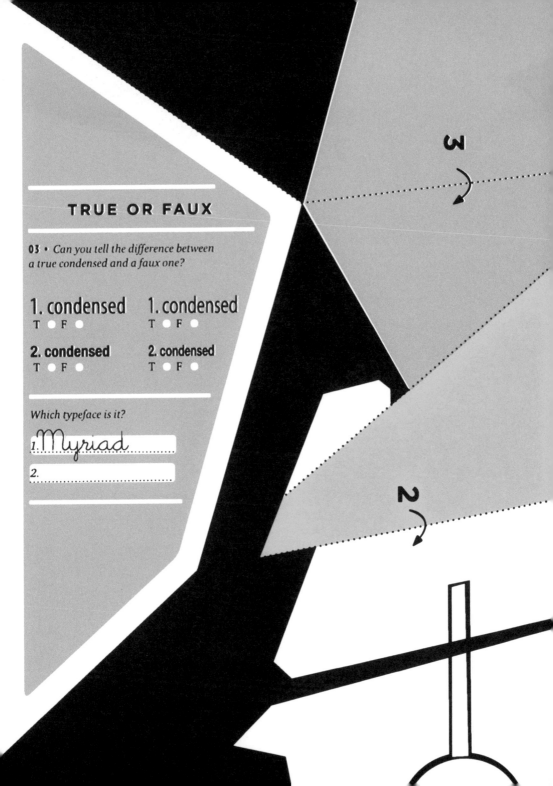

TRUE OR FAUX

03 • *Can you tell the difference between a true condensed and a faux one?*

1. condensed
T ● F ●

1. condensed
T ● F ●

2. condensed
T ● F ●

2. condensed
T ● F ●

Which typeface is it?

1. *Myriad*

2.

3

2

2

FOLD IT

04 • *Fold the paper and see which typographer appears.*

STOP

1

4

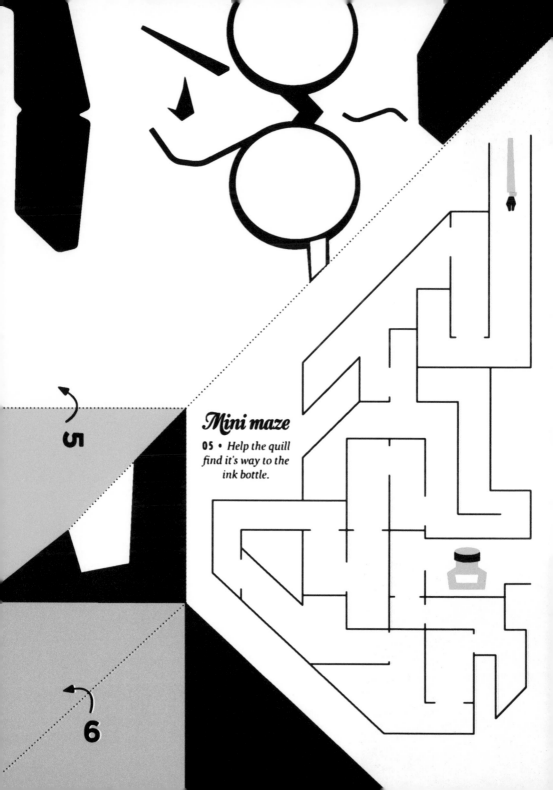

Mini maze

05 • *Help the quill find it's way to the ink bottle.*

P

IS FOR

PARAGRAPH

What other words with a P
can YOU think of?

A typographical term:

....

A typeface:

....

Make your own LIGATURE

P1 • *Make a ligature using the letters: K and I!*

PARTY MASK: 'THE TYPEFACE'

P3 • *Choose a letter from the font of your desire, make a neat face mask and find the costume to go with it! Here are some examples to get you started:*

THE TRAJAN MASK
Great for toga parties.

the Comic Sans mask
Great for children's parties.

P2 • *Which is correct?*

Typography duciuriatem fugiam, officiunt vent haria aut rere, ut unt voloribus, ut ped minti am eaturias autem quiderrum quid eatiat eos voloreped qui debitem poresti onsequi que quaeseque auditate aliquatur autas eos ulluptat as ex esciliqui sequaep ereptat

Correct ☐   Wrong ☐

Typography duciuriatem fugiam, officiunt vent haria aut rere, ut unt voloribus, ut ped minti am eaturias autem quiderrum quid eatiat eos voloreped qui debitem poresti onsequi que quaeseque auditate aliquatur autas eos ulluptat as ex esciliqui sequaep ereptat

Correct ☐   Wrong ☐

Typography duciuriatem fugiam, officiunt vent haria aut rere, ut unt voloribus, ut ped minti am eaturias autem quiderrum quid eatiat eos voloreped qui debitem poresti onsequi que quaeseque auditate aliquatur autas eos ulluptat as ex esciliqui sequaep ereptat urendenis

Correct ☐   Wrong ☐

Typography duciuriatem fugiam, officiunt vent haria aut rere, ut unt voloribus, ut ped minti am eaturias autem quiderrum quid eatiat eos voloreped qui debitem poresti onsequi que quaeseque auditate aliquatur autas eos ulluptat as ex esciliqui sequaep ereptat urendenis

Correct ☐   Wrong ☐

Typography duciuriatem fugiam, officiunt vent haria aut rere, ut unt voloribus, ut ped minti am eaturias autem quiderrum quid eatiat eos voloreped qui debitem poresti onsequi que quaeseque auditate aliquatur autas eos ulluptat as ex esciliqui se-

Correct ☐   Wrong ☐

1:

2:

3:

4:

5:

6:

7:

Beef it up!

P4 • *Fill in the correct name of the delicious letter steaks!*

P5 • *Are you worthy of the 'typographer' title?*
Test your knowledge on this question.

Which of these typefaces did not Morris Fuller Benton design?

A *Bell Gothic*

B *Franklin Gothic*

C *Century Schoolbook*

D *News Gothic*

DOT!

P6 • *The i's dot is a lazy one. It overslept and didn't reach todays meeting. Help the i to get back its dot.*

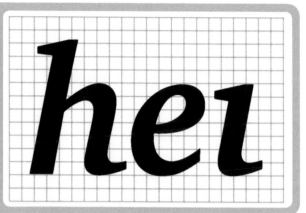

P7 • *The i's cream truck is in the neighbourhood! Unfortunately the i's creams are missing their names. Luckily you have tasted them all before and can help the i's cream truck man write the right names. I's, i's, baby!*

1. ....

2. ....

3. ....

4. ....

5. ....

6. ....

Potatotype

P8 • *Make your own ecological & economic prints!*

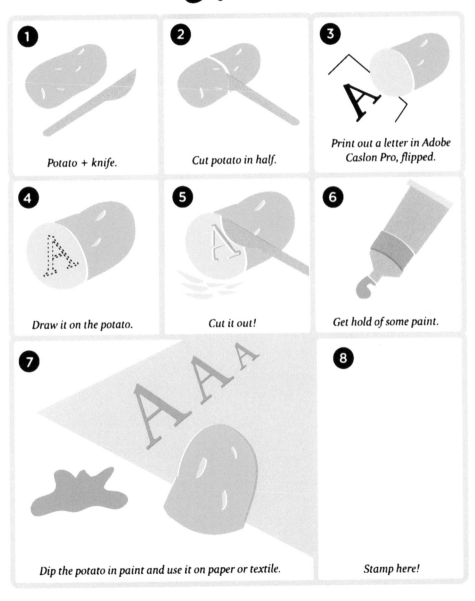

1 Potato + knife.

2 Cut potato in half.

3 *Print out a letter in Adobe Caslon Pro, flipped.*

4 Draw it on the potato.

5 Cut it out!

6 Get hold of some paint.

7 Dip the potato in paint and use it on paper or textile.

8 Stamp here!

GUTENBERG

P9 • *The Gutenberg Bible is one of the first known books printed in Europe. A single complete copy of the bible has 1,272 pages.*

How many pages would the bible have if it was set in Adobe Caslon Pro?

- ○ *850 pages*
- ○ *I don't know...*
- ○ *10 pages*
- ○ *3,250 pages*
- ○ *1,000 pages*
- ○ *Gazillion*

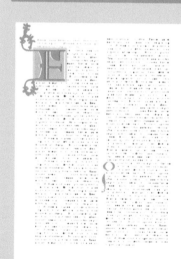

Comic Sans

Garamond

ROSEWOOD

Didot

Zapfino

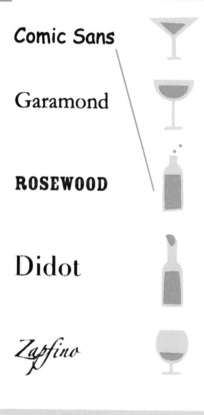

Question mark

P11 • *Which font is this question mark set in?*

Well?

IS FOR

QUOTATION MARK

*What other words with a Q
can YOU think of?*

A typographical term:

....

A typeface:

....

WHO KILLED THE DARLING?

Q1 • *Can you help Detective Type to find the killer? Then read on!*

A HORRIBLE THING HAPPEND LAST NIGHT WHILE TYPOGRAPHERS EVERYWHERE WERE SOUND ASLEEP: ...

... EVERONE'S LOVE-OR-HATE TYPEFACE HELVETICA WAS BRUTALLY MURDERED!

THE CRIME WAS OBVIOUSLY A HATECRIME: STABS, HURTFUL GUNSHOTS, LEAVING THE VICTIM TO SLOWLY BLEED TO DEATH.

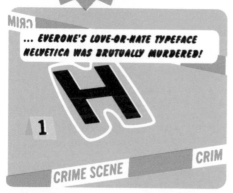

DETECTIVE TYPE HAD SEEN CRIMES LIKE THIS BEFORE, THE MURDERER IS USUALLY SOMEONE KNOWN BY THE VICTIM.

IT WAS SOON REVEALED THAT HELVETICA HAD BEEN TO TYPECON SOME DAYS AGO AND GOT INTO A FIGHT WITH LONG-TIME ENEMIES AKZIDENZ, ARIAL AND UNIVERS.

AFTER CHECKING THEIR ALIBIES, THEY WERE ALL POSSIBLE MURDERERS. NOW THE EVIDENCE WAS THE ONLY THING MISSING. THEN ...

... A FINGERPRINT WAS FOUND ON THE CRIME SCENE AND DETECTIVE TYPE WAS NO LONGER IN DOUBT WHO THE KILLER WAS. CAN YOU GUESS WHO?

REPORT

Fingerprint:

CRAZY COMBINATIONS

Q2 • *This is total chaos. Which typefaces are combined here?*

R   S   V

1. ....
2. ....

1. ....
2. ....

1. ....
2. *Didot*

UPPER CASE STUDY

Q3 • *Which Q do you find most beautiful? Circle your favourite or draw your own!*

Just Kidding

When did typographers get interested in bird watching? When they found out that birds have beaks, too.

GUESS THE NON-TYPOGRAPHICAL TERM!

Q4 • *Can you guess which of the images below doesn't show a typographical term?*

Figure it out!

A   B   C

 # TYPOLYMPICS

X-HEIGHT JUMP

Q5.1 • *Which typeface has the tallest x-height records?*

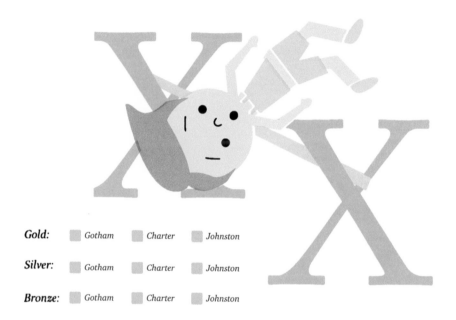

Gold: ▢ Gotham ▢ Charter ▢ Johnston

Silver: ▢ Gotham ▢ Charter ▢ Johnston

Bronze: ▢ Gotham ▢ Charter ▢ Johnston

TYPODIUM

Q5.2 • *Which typefaces got a place on the podium?*

LO

Q5.3 • *Find your typometer and measure h*

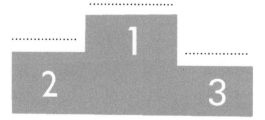

Start

*Jump
stroke*

PARATYPOLYMPICS

Q5.4 • *The handicaps of these letters doesn't keep them from participating in the olympics. What letter parts are missing?*

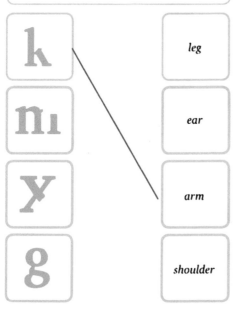

k

n̦

ɣ

g

leg

ear

arm

shoulder

WEIGHT LIFTING

Q5.5 • *Which font lifted the heaviest weight?*

Mr. Caslon Pro Semibold

Mr. Garamond Pro Bold

Mr. Minion Black

MPLINE

ny Picas this competitor jumped!

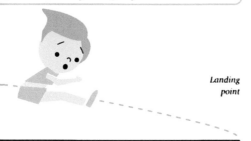

Landing
point

3D-LICIOUS

1 Buy 3D glasses or cardboard and cellophane (red & green) and make your own!

2

3

Q6 • Then study these letters in three dimensions:

ABC

Illustrate a word!

Q7 • Why illustrate with objects when you can illustrate with typography! Let the word illustrate its own meaning! Confused? Our example will help you along.

GREAT EXAMPLE:

VEGETARIAN

Now you try to illustrate:

HAPPY

Awesome!

R

IS FOR

READABILITY

*What other words with an R
can YOU think of?*

A typographical term:

....

A typeface:

....

A. hairy mixup

R1 • *Golly! These typographers are getting old and therefore their memory failed to recognize which wigs belongs to each. Help these old fellas by drawing lines to the right hairstyles!*

1. **2.** **3.**  **4.**

WILLIAM CASLON   **ADRIAN FRUTIGER**   **ALDUS MANUTIUS**   **CLAUDE GARAMOND**

GOTH OR NOT?

R2 • *Which of these letters are known as Gothic?*

DRAW THE LINE!

R3 • *Finish the letter with your pen. It will improve your typographical skills!*

WHAT IS CASLON DREAMING ABOUT?

R4 • *William Caslon is having the most wonderful dream. Connect the fonts chronologically (and alphabetically if fonts are from the same year) and find out what's on his mind!*

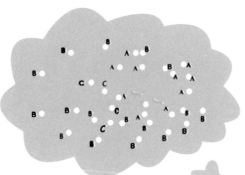

Secretive!

MISSING
FONT

R5 • *Fill in the missing typeface name to complete the rhyme! The description in the poem will guide you in the right direction, so **don't panic!***

*I'm very versatile,
to use me is not a sin.
I'm striking and mechanical,
my name is:*

....

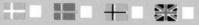

QUOTATION MARKS

R6 • Hi! My name is 'Mark'. I'm a typographer with a good sense of 'humour' and I like to travel. I am soon going on a vacation and I need help to find the typographical 'correct' way to express 'irony' in the different countries.

Ligature or Letter?

R7 • Can you tell the difference between the ligatures and the actual characters? Put a circle around the ligatures.

Æ   Œ   æ   œ   ß

ff   fi   fl   ffi   ffl

ct   st   fh   fi   fl

R8 • Which R do you find most beautiful? Circle your favourite or draw your own!

R R R R

R

Five Senses TASTE

R9 • Which typeface tastes best on this particular kind of paper?

○ Gotham   ○ Garamond

Crack it!

THE SECRET MESSAGE

R10 • Look up the Webdings character set to decode this secret message:

TYPOLOGY

R11 • *Study these type specimens. Can you determine which typefaces they are? Can you also tell which letters they are? Let's zoom in!*

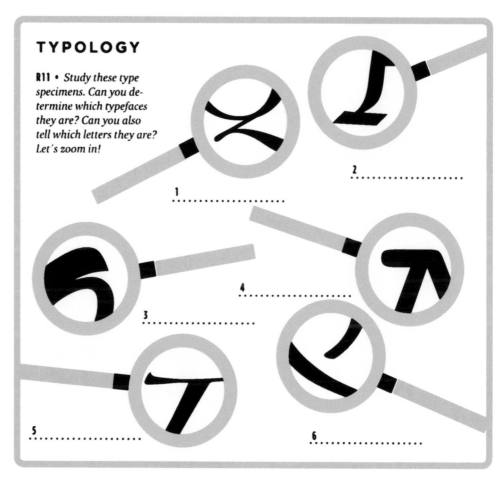

1 ....

2 ....

3 ....

4 ....

5 ....

6 ....

Crazy combinations

R12 • *Here's various specimens that are totally deranged! Which fonts are combined here?*

M

A ....
B ....

K

A ....
B ....

F

A ....
B ....
C ....

S

IS FOR

SANS-SERIF

What other words with an S
can YOU think of?

A typographical term:

....

A typeface:

....

BLOOD TYPE

WHICH BLOOD TYPE IS THE MOST COMMON?

S1 • *Find the order (1 to 4) of commonness for the four blood types A, 0, B and AB based on the popularity of the typefaces swimming in the blood! Don't freak out!*

Ewww!

1: Gotham

NEW H: THE HEALING EFFECT OF TYPE

True!

S2 • *Do you know typefaces can influence your physical and mental health? Here are some typographic remedies for your ills:*

BECOME HAPPIER	**LIVE LONGER**	**BECOME RICH**	**BECOME ORIGINAL**	**FIND GOD**
Use Comic Sans	*Forget about Times*	*Use Bank Gothic*	*Use Eccentric*	*Use Devinne Swash*

X-STITCH

✖ = *pantone 7540 M*

✖ = *pantone 292 M*   ✖ = *pantone 141 M*

1. Choose colour.

2. Follow the x-height.

3. Step and Repeat.

4. Paste text in frame.

COLOUR
JOHN BASKERVILLE

MAKE YOUR OWN POP-UP!

S5 • *Just follow the instructions below:*
1) *Fold the page inward along the dotted line and fold it back.*
2) *Cut along the white lines.*
3) *Fold the top of the word 'hell' and the bottom of the word 'yeah' upward.*
4) *Fold the page outward in the middle at the dotted line where the cutout lettershapes are, leaving the rest.*
5) *Move the left side of the dotted line to stand at a 90 degrees angle. The word should be popping out of the page like in the little illustration (right).*

RORSCHACH

S6 • *Rorschach tests are often used to see what state of mind a patient is in. Which letter(s) do you see and how do you feel about that?*

Impress your friends!!

DRAW THE LETTERS

S7 • *Do you see which letters we miss here? Then draw them in!*

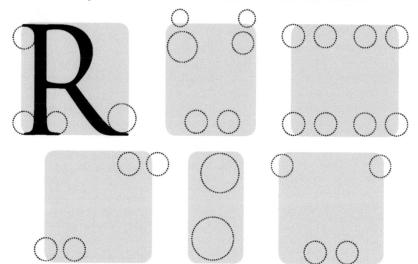

THE KEY ISSUE

S8 • *One of these three keys might open the lock to your typo-graphic career. Simply identify the letter on the lock and open up.*

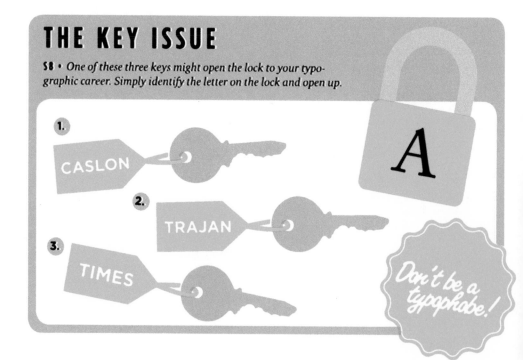

1. CASLON

2. TRAJAN

3. TIMES

A

Don't be a typophobe!

T

IS FOR

TRUETYPE

*What other words with a T
can YOU think of?*

A typographical term:

A typeface:

T1 · TYPE REUNION!

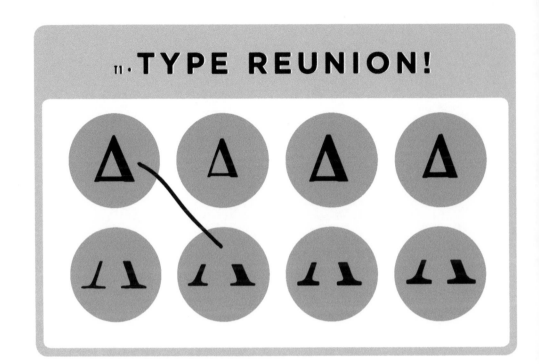

T2 • *Practise your calligraffiti on the train.*

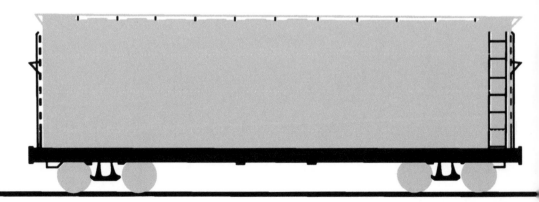

TYPODOKU

Don't panic!

		A	A	A	A	A		A
A	A		A		A		A	A
A			A	A		A		A
A	A	A			A		A	
		A	A		A	A	A	A
	A	A	A	A		A		A
	A	A	A		A		A	
A	A				A	A	A	
A			A	A		A		A

13 • *Fill the empty fields with the nine different typefaces.*
Every row, collumn and square must contain all the fonts.

*- I'm blind!
Help me find my eye!*

Poor thing!

GRAPHOLOGY

T5 • *How good is your friend really? Collect the handwriting of a
friend on the dotted line below and analyze it!*

FRIEND ▶

....

*Now that you have collected the sample, here are the two
factors you should be looking for and what they mean:*

*Emotional energy is measured by looking at
how much pressure the writer has used when
writing.*

Heavy pressure: *A successful typographer,
full of vitality and energy to finely tune his/
her typography and experiment with new
approaches to typography.*
Average pressure: *A moderately successful
typographer. With just enough energy to
make it through the day, there's not a lot of
great typography coming from him/her, but
decent enough.*
Light pressure: *Who? Tries to avoid energy
draining situations and therefore accom-
plishes nothing.*

*Slant of writing is measured by determining
which way the writing slants.*

Right slant: *Is inspired easily by external
forces and is good to motivate him/herself. A
caring, warm and outgoing typographer
whose heart rules the mind and who is deep-
ly passionate and caring about typography.*
Vertical slant (no slant): *Tries to keep
emotion in check. The mind rules the heart.*
Left slant: *Conceals emotions, is cold and
indifferent.*

CRY ME A RIVER

16 • *Find the rivers in this poorly spaced body copy.*

Tincil ulla aliqui bla facing eniscidunt ipsusto consed tion eum nummod magna facidunt praesto duis nonulputat, vel dignim nostrud dolenibh essim quat velenis num aut aci et nosto ea facipis molobore consed magna acipissim illa amet, commodolore venit nullam, vel ullut ut aut eum dolore minibh esed tate min henibh eu faci blaor sectet ut nisit iriliqui bla commy nulputpat, venisl exercillum dolesectem zzriustio odipsuscil ing exerosto do conum ea acinci blandre vullaor erosto doloboreet auguer autetue et iuscillan er iustrud tat veliscing eugait aliquat wiscidunt luptat lobore vel utpate dolore faidui smodignim ea commod estrud tatem velenit nis nonse et amconulla feugiamet venim nullaortie erit wis autem num velit lut lut ut aliquipiscin veliquisl utpat. Duis nosto ea adignim velit utat, veliquat. Oborperosto elis amet aciduis nos dignit aliquat lan ex er sent luptat nit lorem nullutpatet veniat lore venim nostrud moluptatum iriliquipis doluptat. Ut la faci blaorting exerit ut lobore dolore tat, vel utpat. Duisit alit ercipsum niam ad mod ex elisi et nis nonsed tincilit nit vullan ut utat.

17 • *One of Adobe's newest fonts is named after a river. What is the name of this font?*

....

TYPOGRAPHER

18 • *Are you worthy of the 'typographer' title? Test your knowledge on this question.*

Which of these type designers have collaborated?

A *Eric Gill & Edward Johnston*

B *Carol Twombly & Robert Slimbach*

C *William Caslon & Claude Garamond*

D *Paul Rand & Neville Brody*

THE GOLDEN RATIO

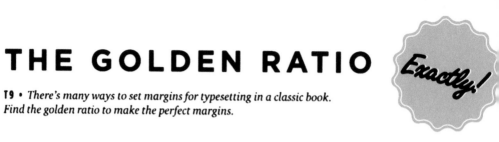

19 • *There's many ways to set margins for typesetting in a classic book.
Find the golden ratio to make the perfect margins.*

1.

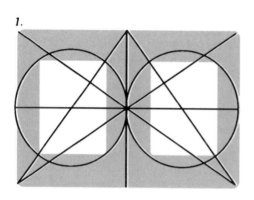

2.

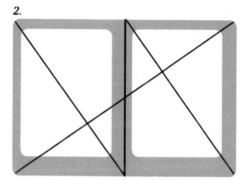

3.

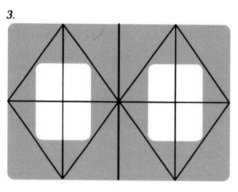

4.

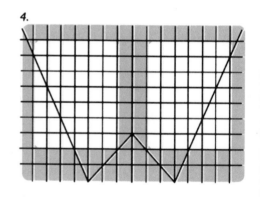

5.

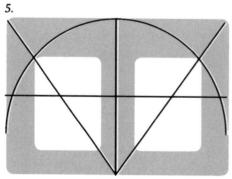

6.

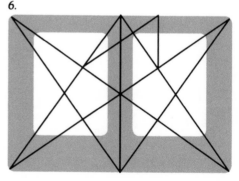

U

IS FOR

UNDERSCORE

*What other words with a U
can YOU think of?*

A typographical term:

....

A typeface:

....

FONT

*I'm quite exclusive
like a filet mignot.
Often used in fashion,
my name is:*

....

U1 • *Fill in the missing typeface to complete the rhyme! The description in the poem will guide you in the right direction, so don't panic!*

Calligraphy

Battle

U2 • *Top the example above!*

Bring it on!

Hierarchy
OF TYPOGRAPHICAL NESECCITIES

U3 • *There are so many typefaces out there that it's hard to figure out which ones you really need. Create some order out of the chaos! Place typefaces in this pyramid according to their level of necessity. Start with the most needed typefaces at the bottom and work your way up to the more flashy, unecessary ones. We have filled in some examples to get you going!*

SELF-ACTUALIZATION

EMOTIONAL NEEDS

Avant Garde

BASIC NEEDS

Myriad   Garamond

Arial   Times New Roman

Push & pull

```
F O L D       A L O N G
T H I     G R E O       M   A K E   E
L E N F   S N   . T H E   E F A     N
A I A A   Y E D N N E .   A C -   A
P L K Y   I S O T E N .   C A     N
L I R E   S S P E A S   H O W
C O U     G       C     I N G
Y O E                   O
T H A                   N
C H A N G E S ?
```

FIND-A-WORD!

U5 • *Fill in the blank spaces to reveal a hidden word!*

........................*wrap*   *font* ....

........................*styles*   .... *rules*

........................*break*   *colour*........................

........................*case*   *proportional*............

base........................   *body*........................

Glyphs Anonymous

U6 • *Who is called what? Fill in the blank name tags or draw the sign in the blank photo frames.*

HELLO my name is

¶ 1

HELLO my name is

diaeresis

HELLO my name is

brevе

HELLO my name is

~

WHOSE HANDWRITING IS THIS?

U7 • *Can you guess who are behind these handwritings?*

1

Belongs to:

....

2

Belongs to:

....

3

My dear Anna

Belongs to:

....

Make snow type!

U8 • *How many letters can you make with your body in the snow? Use your hands and feet to make serifs. For advanced snowletterers; try writing a word!*

DINGBATTLE

U9 • *There are four different symbol typefaces hidden in the image. Can you find the Webdings symbols? Colour them in one distinct colour and a hidden, larger symbol will come forth. Afterwards have fun colouring the rest of the symbols!*

V

IS FOR

VENETIAN

What other words with a V can YOU think of?

A typographical term:

....

A typeface:

....

V1 • *Rorschach tests are often used to see what state of mind a patient is in. Which letter(s) do you see and how do you feel about that?*

V2

NAME THE STYLES

edn

Answer:
....

edn

Answer:
....

edn

Answer:
....

HIDDEN
CHARACTER

V3 • *How well do you know Mr. Baskerville?*

C, O OR G?

GEOTYPOGRAPHY

TYPE AROUND THE WORLD

V4 • *Throughout the book a lot of type-faces have been mentioned. But do you know where they are from? Fill in a type-face name in each of the boxes below.*

From Finland:

....

From Norway:

....

From Sweden:

....

From England:

....

From Germany:

....

From France:

....

From Italy:

....

From Spain:

....

My first font

V5 • *Grab a pen and design your own font! It can be perfect – or totally weird. It's up to you!*

Just Kidding

What did the typographer say when he broke up with his girlfriend? I need more space.

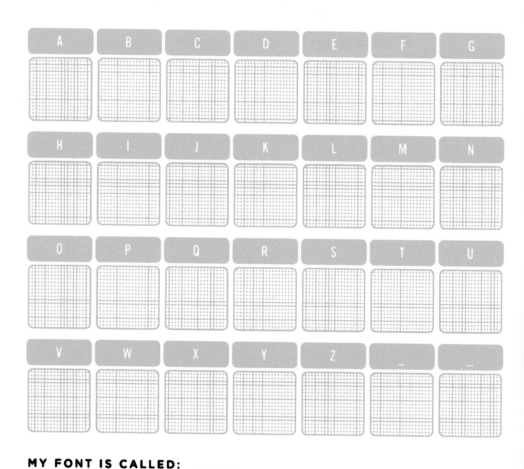

A B C D E F G

H I J K L M N

O P Q R S T U

V W X Y Z _ _

MY FONT IS CALLED: ....

V6 • *Who is crowned as the real Miss Univers?*

V7 • *Are you worthy of the 'typographer' title?*
Test your knowledge on this question.

Which was the first widely adopted sans-serif typeface?

A *Franklin Gothic*

B *Akzidenz Grotesk*

C *Futura*

D *Gill Sans*

HOW FOND OF FONTS ARE YOU?

V8 • *How do you feel about fonts? Do they mean the world to you or could you not care less? This chart will give you the answer! Start at the upper left corner and follow the direction of your answers. It's easy!*

Do you know what a font is?

Yes!

Are you good at spotting the difference between similar fonts?

Yes!

No.

No.

Great! Do you know the exact number of fonts you have on your computer?

Do you at least know the difference between serif and sans-serif?

No.

Yes!

No.

Yes!

Is the number greater than 10,000?

Great! Do you react when people use Comic Sans?

No.

Yes!

Do you consider your fonts an important part of your life?

No.

Yes!

No.

Yes!

You must not like fonts at all! Outrageous!

You are just normally fond of fonts. How boring …

You are on the verge of being addicted to fonts. What would you do without them?

IS FOR

WHITE SPACE

What other words with a W can YOU think of?

A typographical term:

....

A typeface:

....

THE SECRET CODE

W1 • *Which typeface is Detective Type investigating? Help him crack the secret message below by cutting along the dotted lines. Fold the letters and the page inwards to see what the code says!*

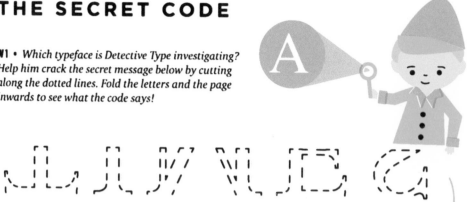

Kamasutra ligatures

W2 • *Pair the ligatures with the right position.*

| SIXTY NINE | SPOON | MISSIONARY | REVERSE SPOON |

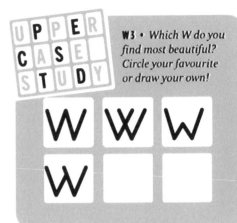

UPPER CASE STUDY

W3 • *Which W do you find most beautiful? Circle your favourite or draw your own!*

W W W
W

THE TYPE MUSEUM

W5 • *Help the museum to gather lost artifacts by drawing typefaces onto the right displays.*

G

Garamond   Caslon

CONTEMPORARY

F

Bauhaus   Futura

OUT OF DATE

C

Comic Sans   Rosewood

TYPOGRAPHIC *manifesto*

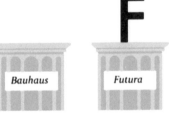

Tough!

W4 • *Which typographical rules do you swear by? Write down your do's/don'ts about kerning, leading, typefaces and so forth. Cut it out and hang it above your desk, so you won't forget!*

MY MANIFESTO:

....
....
....
....
....
....
....
....

Draw yourself!

W6 • *Draw yourself as a professional calligrapher from the 18th century.*

W7 • *How many typographic terms can you make out of the letters in this word:*

HYPERACTIVITYPOGRAPHY

Cap		

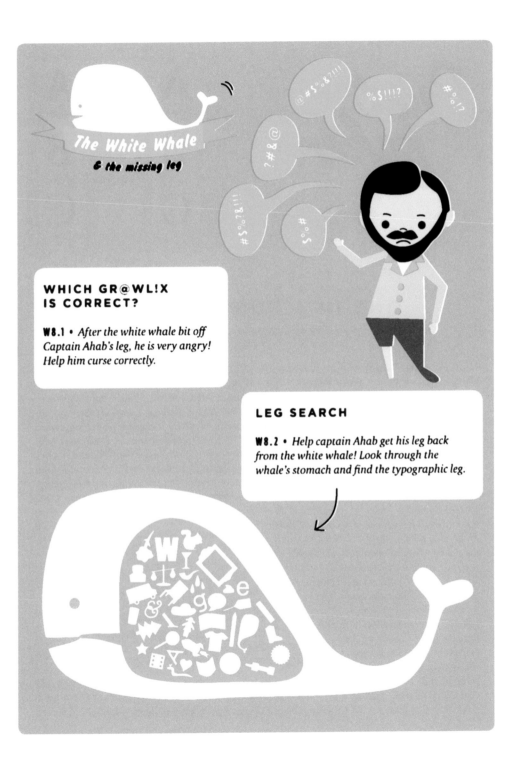

The White Whale
& the missing leg

WHICH GR@WL!X IS CORRECT?

W8.1 • *After the white whale bit off Captain Ahab's leg, he is very angry! Help him curse correctly.*

LEG SEARCH

W8.2 • *Help captain Ahab get his leg back from the white whale! Look through the whale's stomach and find the typographic leg.*

Point faker

A > A
B   B
C   C

W9 • *These fonts are born in different sizes, can you see who has faked some points?*

ONE IN A HUNDRED

W10 • *Can you spot the one and only uncorrect Helvetica version?*

Sort it out!

Helvetica: Light • Light Oblique • Medium • Black • Black Condensed • Black Condensed Oblique • Black Italic • Black Oblique • Black Roman • Bold • Bold Condensed • Bold Condensed Oblique • Bold Italic • Bold Oblique • Bold Roman • Book Italic • Book Roman • Central European Bold • Central European Narrow Bold • Central European Narrow Roman • Central European Roman • (Central European = CE) • Compressed • Compressed Roman • Condensed • Condensed Black Italic • Condensed Black Roman • Condensed Bold Italic • Condensed Bold Roman • Condensed Book Italic • Condensed Book Roman • Condensed Light Italic • Condensed Light Oblique • Condensed Light Roman • Condensed Medium • Condensed Oblique • Condensed Roman • Cyrillic • Cyrillic Bold • Cyrillic Bold Inclined • Cyrillic Inclined • Cyrillic Inserat Upright • Cyrillic Upright • Extra Compressed • Extra Compressed Roman • Fraction • Fraction Bold • Fraction Book • Fractions Medium • Fractions Bold • Greek Bold Inclined • Greek Inclined • Greek Upright • Greek Monotonic Bold • Greek Monotonic Bold Inclined • Greek Monotonic Inclined • Greek Monotonic Upright • Greek Polytonic Bold • Greek Polytonic Bold Inclined • Greek Polytonic Inclined • Greek Polytonic Upright • Inserat • Inserat Cyrillic Upright • Inserat Roman • Light • Light Condensed • Light Condensed Oblique • Light Italic • Light Oblique • Light Roman • Narrow • Narrow Bold • Narrow Bold Italic • Narrow Bold Oblique • Narrow Bold Roman • Narrow Book Italic • Narrow Book Roman • Narrow Oblique • Narrow Roman • Narrow Roman Oblique • Oblique • Roman • Roman Oblique • Rounded Black • Rounded Black Oblique • Rounded Bold • Rounded Bold Oblique • Rounded Bold Condensed • Rounded Bold Condensed Oblique • Textbook Bold • Textbook Bold Oblique • Textbook Roman • Textbook Roman Oblique • Textbook Light • Ultra Compressed • Ultra Compressed Roman Helvetica Neue: 23 UltraLight Extended • 23 Ultra Light Extended Oblique • 25 Ultra Light • 26 Ultra Light Italic • 27 Ultra Light Condensed • 27 Ultra Light Condensed Oblique • 33 Thin Extended • 33 Thin Extended Oblique • 35 Thin • 36 Thin Italic • 37 Thin Condensed • 37 Thin Condensed Oblique • 43 Light Extended • 43 Light Extended

X

IS FOR

X-HEIGHT

What other words with an X can YOU think of?

A typographical term:

....

A typeface:

....

TYPE FACE

X1 • *Match the face with a typeface!*

ROSEWOOD

Minion

Chaparral

Comic Sans

Eramatch!

X2 • *Which typefaces matches which era?*

A

1. Rome BC

B

2. ....

m

3. ....

E

4. ....

P

5. ....

C

6. ....

N

7. ....

E

8. ....

1. Middle Ages	3. Modernism	5. 1800's	7. 1920's
2. Renaissance	4. Bauhaus	6. Rome BC	8. 21st Century

My dear! Ever since I set my eyes on you for the first time, I thought you were perfect. Yes, I simply think you're the best. I can offer you a good life and a pretty house by the fjord.

LOVE LETTER

X3 • *Find the letters that have the potential to become a ligature pair.*

QUILLARIOUS

X4 • *Connect the quill tip to the text it has calligraphed:*

Neat!

Neat!

Neat!

FINISH THE SENTENCE!

Right on!

X5 • *Which type designer's work was at one point so popular that the following expression was introduced:*

'WHEN IN DOUBT, USE ...:

. . . .

Just Kidding

Why's the typographer's wife jealous? Because, when he texted her: 'I love U', he actually meant that, literally.

Foreign Affairs

X6.1 • *Find out how to write your name in a foreign alphabet. Write it here:*

. . . .

X6.2 • *Which typeface is this?*

- Hiragino Kaku Gothic
- Kozuka Gothic Pro
- Osaka
- ST Heiti

X6.3 • *Use a quill and try copy the Arabic word below as best as you can. Do you actually know what the word means?*

COLOUR BY FONT:
FOREIGN EDITION

X6.4 • *How well do you know the fonts listed below? You'll find a symbol from each font in the image which should be coloured with a particular colour, as seen below. The colouring will reveal a beautiful exotic letter. And it will be beautifully coloured too!*

- LiHei Pro
- Hiragino Mincho
- Apple LiGothic

WHEN & WHAT?

X6.5 • *Who of us has the oldest alphabet?*

ARABIC:
- [ ] 500 BC
- [ ] 450 BC
- [ ] 400 BC

CHINESE:
- [ ] 1200 BC
- [ ] 950 BC
- [ ] 125 BC

HEBREW:
- [ ] 800 BC
- [ ] 300 BC
- [ ] 100 AD

▲

I HEART YOU

X6.6 • *What countries are in their hearts?
Find out which language the red symbols belong
to and fill in country names on the dotted lines.*

WHO WRITES WHAT?

X6.7 • *Which belongs together? Can you
tell the difference?*

CORRECT THIS!

X7 • *Can you see which corrections have been made? Circle the corrections in the after-image.*

ORIGAMI
- IT'S FUN & SIMPLE!

X8 • *Study the shapes and make your own origami alphabet!*

ABC

PAPER CUT

X9 • *Get in touch with your emotions. Get yourself a papercut and write down what you feel.*

Ouch!

The typographer has received a layout he is to correct - and he has to do it fast, the deadline is at 5:30 PM and he worries he won't finish in time!
Now, there are several things wrong with the piece. Compare the text in the image below to this one. Can you see the corrections he has made? There are seven corrections waiting to be spotted. Some are quite tiny, so put your mind to typography mode. Don't worry, you'll do great!

The typographer has received a layout he is to correct – and he has to do it fast, the deadline is at 5:30 PM and he worries he won't finish in time!

Now, there are several things wrong with the piece. Compare the text in the image below to this one. Can you see the corrections he has made? There are seven corrections waiting to be spotted. Some are quite tiny, so put your mind to typography mode. Don't worry, you'll do great!

Y

IS FOR
YOU TO DECIDE

We couldn't think of anything,
but can YOU think of something?

A typographical term:

....

A typeface:

....

EXTREME MAKEOVER

Y1 • *Some letters are addicted to cosmetic surgery. What if you give such an operation a serious try yourself?*

An example to begin with:

BEFORE

A

AFTER

A

Now you do it!

BEFORE

B

AFTER

For real.

CRAZY PUZZLE!

Y2 • *Cut out the puzzle and discover which mystical letter appears. Or is it actually a letter?…*

Spaced out!

Y3.1 • *Use your typographer's eye to guess the spacing, then use the typometer (in the front of this book) to get a correct measurment. It's fascinating!*

1 Spacing · *My guess:* 75 · · · · · · *My measurement:* 100

2 Spacing · *My guess:* · · · · · · · · · · *My measurement:*

3 S p a c i n g · *My guess:* · · · · · · · · · · *My measurement:*

4 Spacing · *My guess:* · · · · · · · · · · *My measurement:*

LETTER SEARCH

Y3.2 • *Where was Futura the first font to go to? Find the F's written in Futura in the font chaos and follow the numbered points until the image is complete!*

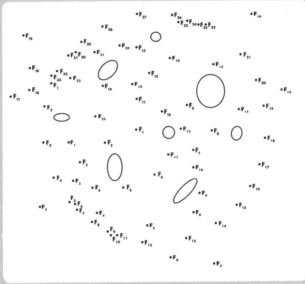

Y3.3 • *The first manned mission to the the moon, Apollo 11, left a plaque where Futura was used. Can you find Futura in the font samples below?*

SEE THE FUTURA!

Apollo 11	**Apollo 11**	Apollo 11
Apollo 11	Apollo 11	Apollo 11
Apollo 11	Apollo 11	Apollo 11
Apollo 11	Apollo 11	Apollo 11

BEFORE & AFTER

Y4 • *Here we see two samples of Helvetica and Helvetica Neue. Who is who? Can you tell the difference? Check off the one you think came first!*

ABC
Hamburgefons

☐ THIS CAME FIRST!

ABC
Hamburgefons

☐ THIS CAME FIRST!

Phat cool!

WEIGHTWATCHERS

1   5   10   15

Y5 • *Not all fonts look the same weight when set in regular; some look fat, some look slim. Figure out which weight the fonts below are set in! Draw an arrow to point to the right answer.*

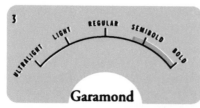

1
ULTRALIGHT · LIGHT · REGULAR · SEMIBOLD · BOLD
Gill Sans

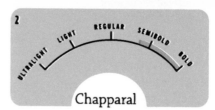

2
ULTRALIGHT · LIGHT · REGULAR · SEMIBOLD · BOLD
Chapparal

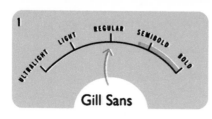

3
ULTRALIGHT · LIGHT · REGULAR · SEMIBOLD · BOLD
Garamond

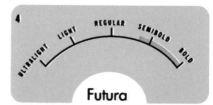

4
ULTRALIGHT · LIGHT · REGULAR · SEMIBOLD · BOLD
Futura

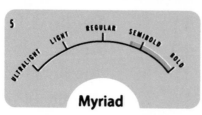

5
ULTRALIGHT · LIGHT · REGULAR · SEMIBOLD · BOLD
Myriad

6
ULTRALIGHT · LIGHT · REGULAR · SEMIBOLD · BOLD
Century Gothic

PASTE IN PLACE

Y6 • Fill in the typeface names in the correct place to understand the story.

Once upon a [   ] there was an [   ] who wanted to travel to another [   ], but he crashed into a [   ] and instead of going to the [   ] he ended up in the big [   ].

American Typewriter

Copperplate

Century

Univers

Times

Futura

HERB
LUBALIN

Homage

TO A
TYPE DESIGNER

Y7 • Pay a tribute to the designer above. It can be inspired by his personality, his typefaces or something entirely different. Be playful!

Y8 • *Are you worthy of the 'typographer' title? Test your knowledge on this question.*

What is a TrueType?

A A person staying true to his/her character

B A very honest, truthful person.

C A new blood type that fits everyone.

D An outline font standard.

THE FONT
yearbook

Y9 • *Decide which glyphs are most likely to receive the yearbook titles!*

COUPLE OF THE YEAR

MOST LIKELY TO SUCCEED

THE SQUARE

THE NERD

THE ARTIST

THE GOTH

CLASS CLOWN

THE GEEK

Z

IS FOR

ZZZ...

*What words with a Z
can YOU think of?*

A typographical term:

....

A typeface:

....

Fontasize

21 • *Finish the story in as many words you like.*

The quick brown fox jumped over the lazy dog. Then

....

....

....

....

....

....

....

....

....

HAPPY BIRTH- DAY, MYRIAD!

22 • *It's Myriad's Birthday! Find out how many years this rad font is by counting the candles on the cake.*
Age: ....

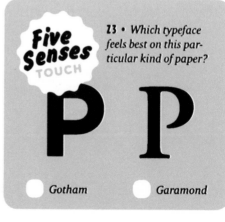

23 • *Which typeface feels best on this particular kind of paper?*

Five Senses TOUCH

P   P

◯ Gotham   ◯ Garamond

DRAW THE LETTER STROKE!

24

a b c d e

Crazy puzzles!

25 • *Solve these typographical rebuses.*

Verbalise!

Letterpress pillow

1. Sew the shortside of C together with shortside B.
2. After sewing together all sides, sew the remaining part to the 'halfbox'. Leave one side open.
3. Stuff the pillow and sew the last side.
4. You can choose any letter you want. Below is an example with T.

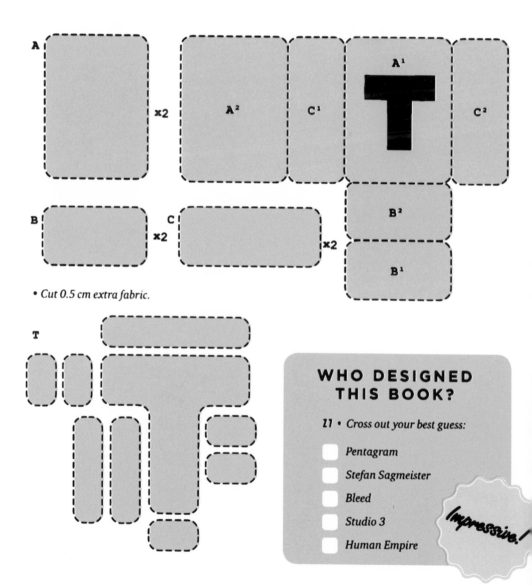

A   x2

A²

C¹

A¹

C²

B²   B¹

B   x2

C   x2

• Cut 0.5 cm extra fabric.

T

Fontsight test!

Use the typometer to mesure and write the size here in points:

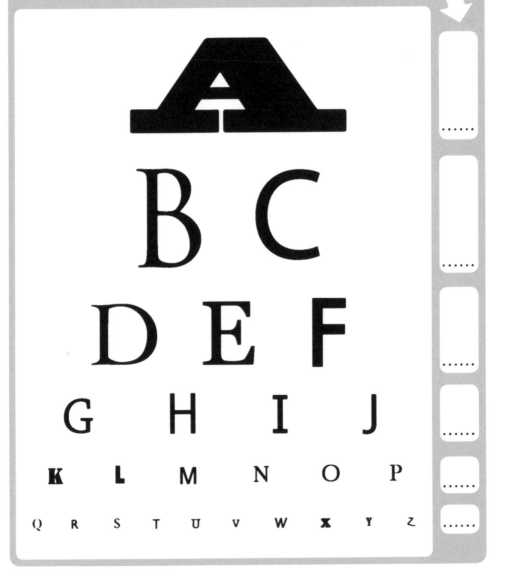

A

......

B C

......

D E F

......

G H I J

......

K L M N O P

......

Q R S T U V W X Y Z

......

QUILL & PAPER

29 • *Get some ink on your quill and finish the text:*

BLACK LETTER

𝔜ou and

UNCIAL

God

COPPERPLATE

Mother

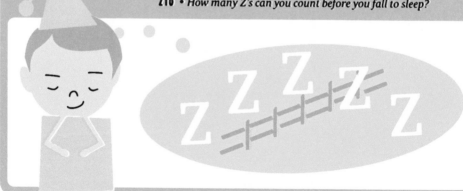

210 • *How many Z's can you count before you fall to sleep?*

!
IS FOR
ANSWERS

A2 • $V+V=W$
$W \cdot 180° = M$
$A+(O \cdot 0,1) = \mathring{A}$
$O^2 = 8$

A3 •

FATHER — son
FATHER — son
FATHER — son
FATHER — son
FATHER — son

A4 •

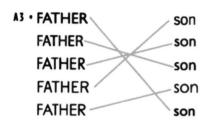

shoulder · head · leg · foot

A5 •

1. *Italic*   (*1. Italic*) = Adobe Garamond
T □ F □

2. Italic   (2. Italic) = Futura
T □ F □

(3. Italic)   3. Italic = Helvetica Neue
T □ F □   T □ F □

(4. Italic)   4. Italic = Arno
T □ F □   T □ F □

A6 •

Arial

A7 •

A8 • *Fox:*

S	N	E	B	S	X	Q
M	W	U	E	P	O	U
I	O	T	X	M	F	I
L	R	H	B	U	A	C
I	B	E	Z	J	Z	K

Dog:

D	R	E	V	O	R	M
O	J	E	H	T	L	W
G	D	P	P	A	K	J
L	F	L	Z	Z	D	U
X	R	Y	T	V	H	P

A9 • A: Comic Sans and American Typewriter.
B: Stencil and Times.
X: Adobe Caslon Pro and Georgia.

A10 •

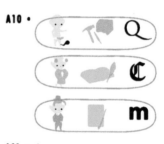

A11 • *A*

B1 • 1 + B
2 + F
3 + D
4 + A
5 + C
6 + E

B2 • *It's Helvetica's birthday! Helvetica was designed by Max Miedinger in Switzerland.*

B6 • *Baskerville.*

B7 • *B: Adobe Jenson Bold.*

B8 • *Nose is not a typographical term.*

B9 •

B10 •

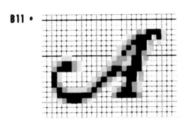

B11 •

Adobe Caslon Pro Italic A with swashes.

B13 • *Bell Gothic.*

CHAPTER C

C4 • *The bogus glyph:* ğ

C5 • *Least equal: The second 'equal' is the least equal font, written in Optima. While the other fonts are typical sans-serif fonts, Optima has the look of a 'serifless roman' with its classically roman letterforms.*

C6 •

C8 •

C12 •

CHAPTER D

D6.1 • *67 pts.*

D6.2 • *21*

D6.3 • *Bell Gothic, Rosewood, Baskerville, Optima.*

D6.5 • *1: Free (Aller).*
2: $29 (Helvetica).
3: $35 (Garamond).

D6.6 • *Robert Bringhurst.*

D6.7 • *A: False.*
B: False.
C: True.

D6.8 • *All of the above.*

D7 • *Typography.*

D8 • *Caslon (6) = Garamond (6).*
Myriad (42) > Helvetica Std (19).
Bickham Script (3) > Zapfino (1).
Times (4) < Times New Roman (7).
Futura (24) > Avant Garde (20).

D9 • *1: Herculanum.*
2: Egyptienne.
3: Univers.
4: OCR-B.
5: Rusticana.

E1 •

Word spacing	**>**	Character spacing
Line spacing	**>**	Word spacing
Character spacing	**<**	Line spacing

E2 •

LET'S FIND THE TYPO GRAPHER

E7 •

E
B
F

E8 • *Francois Didot.*
John Baskerville.
Claude Garamond.
William Caslon.
Giambattista Bodoni.

E9 • *Eric Gill.*

E10 • Helvetica

E11 • *Bottom left, because it's six points bigger!*

E12 •

E13 •

NEVERMORE

E14 • Find the hidden ambigram

You are doing great!

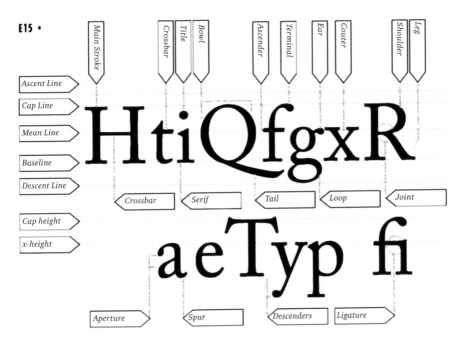

Main Stroke · Crossbar · Title · Bowl · Ascender · Terminal · Ear · Counter · Shoulder · Leg

Ascent Line
Cap Line
Mean Line
Baseline
Descent Line

Cap height
x-height

HtiQfgxR

Crossbar · Serif · Tail · Loop · Joint

aeTyp fi

Aperture · Spur · Descenders · Ligature

CHAPTER F

F4 • M

F5 • 1: Tahoma.
2: Andale Mono.
3: Arial.
4: Helvetica.
5: Gill Sans.
6: Myriad.
7: Bell Gothic.
8: Futura.
9: Verdana.
10: Letter Gothic.
11: Trebuchet.
12: News Gothic.

F6 • It's a trick question! American Typewriter is not used, but the typewriter itself is of an American brand.

F7 • ABCabc

F8 • 3000 BC: Paper (papyrus).
700 BC: Latin alphabet.
1398: Johannes Gutenberg.
1450: Moveable type.
1455: The book.
1490: Claude Garamond.
1501: Italic.
1882: Eric Gill.
1928: Adrian Frutiger.
1959: Carol Twombly.
1996: OpenType.
1999: InDesign.

F9 • Lower case and small caps.

F10 • Ephram Edward Benguia.

F11 •   = *Futura*.

2. Bold **2. Bold** = *Bauhaus*.

3. Bold **3. Bold** = *Adobe Caslon*.

4. Bold **4. Bold** = *Georgia*.

F13 • *D*

CHAPTER G

G1 •

Gill Sans belongs to Eric Gill.
Johnston ITC belongs to Edward Johnston.

G2 • $a + e = æ$
$N \cdot 90° = Z$
$(=) + L = E$
$C + \mathsf{O} = S$

G4 • *1: Hoefler Text by Hoefler & Frere J.*
2: DIN by FontFont.
3: EdPs by House Ind.
4: Cholla Slab Ultra Bold by Emigre.
5: Aardwark by Font Bureau.

G5 • $I = 1$ $II = 2$
$V = 5$ $IV = 4$
$X = 10$ $IX = 9$
$L = 50$ $LVI = 56$
$C = 100$ $XXI = 21$
$D = 500$ $MXIV = 1014$
$M = 1000$ $MCMXCIX = 1999$

G7 • *Frederic Goudy.*

G8 • *The Fashion Designer – Didot.*
The Carpenter – Copperplate.
The Barber – Rosewood.
The Disc Jockey – Eurostile.
The Painter – Brush Script.

G10 • *Hand.*

G11 • *First row, third column (American Typewriter).*

G12 • *Doesn't use Gill Sans: iMac, Underground, Lucky Strike, Subway and Chanel.*

CHAPTER H

H1 •

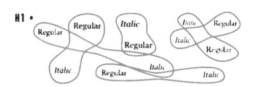

H2 • *Regular.*

H3 • *Bullet.*

H5 •

H6 •

ABCDEFGH
abcdefgh

FATHER   son
FATHER   son
FATHER   son
FATHER   son
FATHER   son

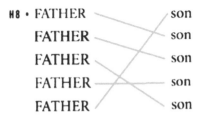

H9 • *Which typeface are you: Test results*

MOST A'S: YOU ARE HELVETICA
You're pretty standard, borderlining boring. To many this means you are reliable and a friend to trust. It's easy to like you! You don't have a lot of opinions and go with the crowd, blending in everywhere. But some people find your lack of personality annoying and can't stand you because of it.

MOST B'S: YOU ARE GARAMOND
You are elegant and timeless. Some might consider you a snob due to your high standards: You expect nothing less than top quality and refuse to be seen with just anyone. Where you are, perfection follows. Your taste is flawless, you are well respected, eloquent and of true value.

MOST C'S: YOU ARE COURIER
You like things down-to-earth and real, rather than trendy and technological. You go against the crowd and are your own person, staying true to your principles and never compromising. Some might say you are stuck in the past, but other's opinions have never bothered you. You keep a lot to yourself and prefer it that way.

MOST D'S: YOU ARE COMIC SANS
The kid inside you is alive and kicking. Some might consider you to be ridiculously immature and think you have some growing up to do. Just like Comic Sans you are annoying to many, but eternally loved by some, usually people as childish as yourself.

MOST E'S: YOU ARE WEBDINGS
You're a weird one, and misunderstood by most people; to them you speak in codes. They might find you superfluous, but that's just because they haven't taken time to get to know you and therefore haven't discovered your potential yet.

CHAPTER I

11 •

12 • *Orphan.*

13 •

15 •

16 • *Futura.*

I7 • Bottom left. because it's bold.

I9 • Robert Slimbach.

I10.1 •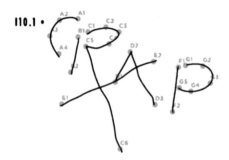

I10.2 •

I11 • Robert Slimbach.

I12 • The glyphs I, l and 1 set in Gill Sans.

CHAPTER J

J1 • Did you know this is written in 3 pt.?

J2 • 1+B
2+E
3+A
4+C
5+D

J3 • Team Arial.

J4 •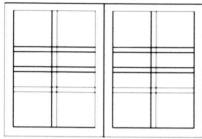

J5 • Myriad Semibold.

J7 •

J8 • William Caslon.

J9 • Dizzy.

J10 • 1: Caslon 15 times.
2: Helvetica 13 times.
3: Times 8 times.
4: Garamond 6 times.
5: Akzidenz Grotesk 5 times.

J11 • Cap.
Drop cap.
Eye.
Ear.
Chin.
Arm.
Body.
Hairline.
Leg.
Footnote.
Feet.

Bleed.
Bullett.
Overshoot.
Woodtype.
Beak.
Path.
Quick brown fox.
Grave.
Thorn.
Shoulder.

L3 • *B*

L4 • *Baskerville =*

    Adobe Jenson Pro =

    Adobe Caslon Pro =

    Arno Pro =

    Brioso Pro =

CHAPTER K

K4 •

L6 • *Hoefler Text:* **D**

L7 • *ff, ffi, ꜩ, ſt, fi, æ.*

K7 • *The hyphens should be dashes.*

L10 • *Layout 1: Renaissance.*
    Layout 2: Bauhaus.
    Layout 3: Modernism.
    Layout 4: Baroque.

K9 • *The left one is faux italic.*

CHAPTER L

CHAPTER M

M2 •

FATHER — son
FATHER — son
FATHER — son
FATHER — son
FATHER — son

L1 • *B*

1. TYPE
U C ✓

1. TYPE
U ✓ C ✗ = *Trebuchet*

2. TYPE
U C ✗

2. TYPE
U ✓ C ✗ = *Myriad*

3. TYPE
U C ✗

3. TYPE
U ✓ C ✓ = *Fedra*

4. TYPE
U ✗ C ✓

4. TYPE
U C ✗ = *Adobe Caslon*

M3 •

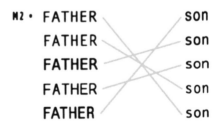

M4.1 • *3*

M4.2 • 'Neque porro
quisquam est qui do-
lorem ipsum quia dolor
sit amet, consectetur,
adipisci velit...'

Translated: 'There is no one who loves pain
itself, who seeks after it and wants to have
it, simply because it is pain…'

M4.3 • *1500s.*

M4.4 • *C*

M7 • *Impact.*

M9.1 • *Norway and Denmark.*

M9.2 • *Æsthetics.*

M9.3 • *Option + i.*

M9.4 • *A + E*

M9.5 • *a + e*

M11 • Sub₁ (Sub₁) = *Adobe Caslon*
T ☐ F ☐   T ☐ F ☐

Sub₂ (Sub₂) = *Adobe Garamond*
T ☐ F ☐   T ☐ F ☐

Super³ (Super³) = *Futura*
T ☐ F ☐   T ☐ F ☐

CHAPTER N

N1 • *In Garamond's lap:*

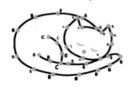

N2 • *Jan Tchischold.*

N3 • *1: Adobe Garamond.*
2: Rosewood.

N5 • *1+B*
2+C
3+A

N6 • Arial
Designed in 1982 by Robin Nicholas
and Patricia Saunders for Monotype (not
Microsoft), it's classified as Neo Grotesque, was originally called Sonoran San
Serif, and was designed for IBM's bitmap
font laser printers.

It was first supplied with Windows 3.1 (1992)
and was one of the core fonts in all subsequent versions of Windows until Vista,
when to all intents and purposes, it was
replaced with Calibri.

Helvetica
Designed in 1957 by Max Miedinger,
Helvetica's design is based on that of
Akzidenz Grotesk (1896), and classified as
a Grotesque / Transitional sans-serif face.

Originally it was called Neue Haas Grotesque; in 1960 it was revised and
renamed Helvetica (Latin for Switzerland
"Swiss").

N7 • *Em space.*

N10 • *Optic Illusion.*

N11 • *Roman.*
Spur.
Lazy dog.
Bar.
Counter.
Bowl.
Pipe.
Justify.
Family.
Light.
Book.
Table.
Case.
Currency symbol.

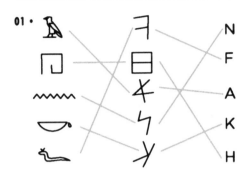

01 •

02 • Trajan.

03 • 1. condensed   1. condensed = Myriad Pro
    T F   T F

    2. condensed   2. condensed = Helvetica Neue
    T F   T F

04 • Eric Gill.

P2 • *T**ypography duciuriatem fugiam, officiunt vent haria aut rere, ut unt voloribus, ut ped minti am eaturias autem quiderrum quid eatiat eos voloreped qui debitem poresti onsequi que quaeseque auditate aliquatur autas eos ulluptat as ex esciliqui sequaep ereptat*

P4 • 1: Head serif.
    2: Main stroke.
    3: Foot serif.
    4: Shoulder.
    5: Joint.
    6: Leg.
    7: Tail.

P5 • A

P6 • *hei*

P7 • 1: Rosewood
    2: American Typewriter.
    3: Courier.
    4: Garamond.
    5: Trajan.
    6: Bell Gothic.

P9 • Gazillion.

P10 •

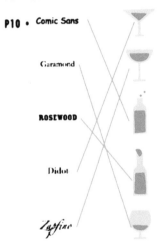

P11 • Gill Sans Regular.

Q1 • Arial.

Q2 • R: Rosewood and Cooper Black.
    S: Courier and Chapparal Pro.
    V: Didot and Futura.

Q4 • A: Cheek.

Q5.1 • *Gold: Gotham.*
Silver: Charter.
Bronze: Johnston.

Q5.2 • *1: Futura.*
2: Gill Sans.
3: Univers.

Q5.4 •

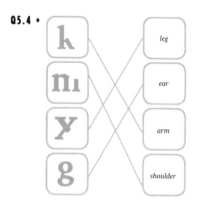

Q5.5 • *Mr. Minion Black.*

R1 • *1: Aldus Manutius.*
2: Claude Garamond.
3: William Caslon.
4: Adrian Frutiger.

R2 • *The two first letters are known as gothic:*

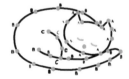

R4 • *Caslon's dream:*

R5 • *DIN.*

R6 • *Norway, Demark, Sweden, England.*

R7 • *All of them.*

R10 • *'Now you have translated it.*
Good for you.'

R11 • *1: Baskerville, Q.*
2: Apple Chancery, F.
3: Brush Script, O.
4: Courier, A.
5: Zapfino, K.
6: Herculanum, Q.

R12 • *M : Myriad and Tekton Pro.*
K: Lithos Pro and Herculanum.
F: Adobe Caslon Pro, Arial and
Baskerville.

S1 • *A: Gotham.*
B: Comic Sans.
O: Garamond.
AB: Helvetica.

S7 •

S8 • *Caslon.*

T1 •

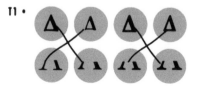

T3 •

T4 •

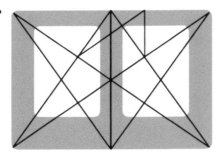

T8 • B

T9 •

CHAPTER U

U1 • Didot.

U5 • Text wrap, paragraph styles, line break, lower case, base line, font family, paragraph rules, colour settings, proportional figures, body copy.

U6 • *1:* ¶ = pilcrow
2: diaeresis = ¨
3: breve = ˘
4: ~ = tilde

U7 • *1: Albert Einstein.*
2: Leonardo DaVinci.
3: Jane Austen.

U9 •

CHAPTER V

V2 • *Garalde.*
Didone.
Transitional.

V3 •

C
O
G

V6 •

V7 • B

CHAPTER W

W1 ·

W2 ·

W8.1 · @#$%&?!!!

W8.2 ·

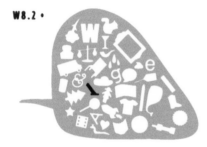

W9 ·

A	>	A
B	<	B
C	>	C

W10 · *Textbook Light.*

CHAPTER X

X1 · *Comic Sans.*

X2 · *1: Rome BD.*
2: Bauhaus.
3: Modernism.

4: 1800s.
5: 1920s.
6: Middle Ages.
7: 21st Century.
8: Renaissance.

X3 ·

X4 · *My dear! Ever since I set my eyes on you for the first time, I thought you were perfect. Yes, I simply think you're the best. I can offer you a good life and a pretty house by the fjord.*

X5 · *... Caslon.*

X6.2 · *Kozuka Gothic Pro.*

X6.2 · *The Arabic word means 'Exotic'.*

X6.4 ·

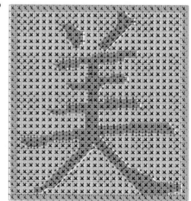

X8.5 • *Arabic: 400 BC.*
Chinese: 1200 BC.
Hebrew: 300 BC.
The Chinese character set is the oldest.

X6.6 • *China and Israel.*

X6.7 •

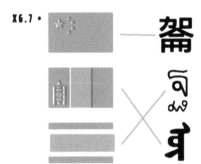

X7 • *Ligatures (Th and fi), dash, old style fig-*
ures, capital letters, indent, baseline.

The typographer has received a layout he is to correct – and he has to do it fast, the deadline is at 5:30 PM and he worries he won't finish in time!

Now, there are several things wrong with the piece. Compare the text in the image below to this one. Can you see the corrections he has made? There are seven corrections waiting to be spotted. Some are quite tiny, so put your mind to typography mode. Don't worry, you'll do great!

CHAPTER Y

Y1 •

A A B B

Y2 • &

Y3.1 • *1: 100*
2: 25
3: 200
4: –25

Y3.2 •

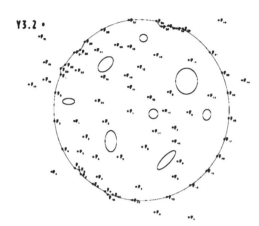

Y3.3 •

Apollo 11   **Apollo 11**   Apollo 11
Apollo 11   Apollo 11   (Apollo 11)
Apollo 11   Apollo 11   Apollo 11
Apollo 11   Apollo 11   Apollo 11

Y4 • *The Helvetica to the left came first.*

Y5 • *1: Gill Sans Regular.*
2: Chaparral Light.
3: Garamond Semibold.
4: Futura Medium.
5: Myriad Semibold.
6: Century Gothic Regular.

Y6 • *Once upon a times there was an american*
typewriter who wanted to travel to another
century, But he crashed into a copperplate
and instead of going to the futura he ended
up in the big univers.

Y8 • *D*

CHAPTER Z

Z2 • *18*

Z4 •

25 • 1: *American Typewriter.*
2: *Rockwell.*

27 • *Studio 3.*

28 • 1: *Blackoak.*
2: *Trajan Pro.*
3: *Myriad.*
4: *Cochin.*
5: *Georgia.*
6: *Futura.*
7: *Chapparal Pro.*
8: *News Gothic.*
9: *Verdana.*
10: *Lucida Grande.*
11: *Stencil.*
12: *Poplar.*
13: *Helvetica.*
14: *Times.*
15: *Optima.*
16: *Baskerville.*
17: *Didot.*
18: *Gill Sans.*
19: *Hoefler Text.*
20: *Arial.*
21: *American Typewriter.*
22: *Courier.*
23: *Comic Sans.*
24: *Cooper Black.*
25: *Rosewood.*
26: *Herculanum.*

Five Senses & 1 SIXTH SENSE

15 • *Can you see the dead typographer on this particular kind of paper?*

◯ *I see him!*   ◯ *I don't see him!*

Yay! Well done!

■ ■ ■
IS FOR
PRACTICE!

DOODLE: SCRIPT

Ascender line

Cap line

Mean line

Baseline

Descender line

Ascender line

Cap line

Mean line

Baseline

Descender line

Ascender line

Cap line

Mean line

Baseline

Descender line

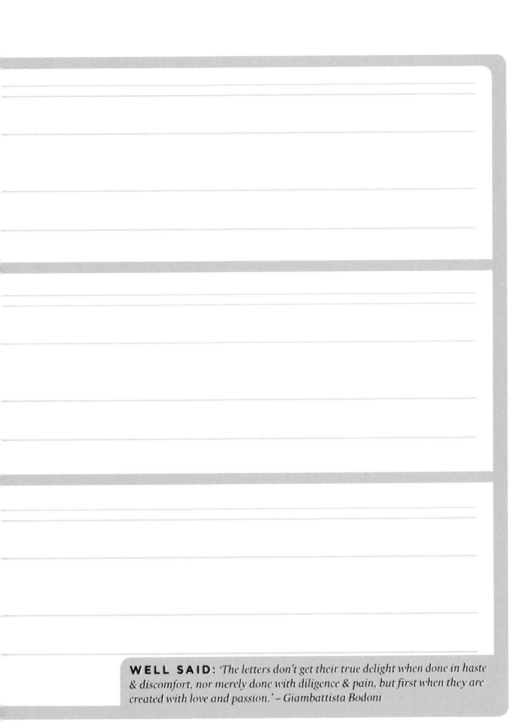

WELL SAID: *'The letters don't get their true delight when done in haste & discomfort, nor merely done with diligence & pain, but first when they are created with love and passion.' – Giambattista Bodoni*

DOODLE: SCRIPT

Ascender line
Cap line

Mean line

Baseline

Descender line

Ascender line
Cap line

Mean line

Baseline

Descender line

Ascender line
Cap line

Mean line

Baseline

Descender line

WELL SAID: *'In the fields of Printing & Graphic Design, it is generally agreed that the poet in our midst is the type designer.'* – Noel Martin

You did it!

DIPLOMA

*In recognition of the successful completion of the activities in this book,
the Institute of Hyperactivitypography hereby officially declares*

(your name)

AUTHORIZED BUT NEVERTHELESS AWESOME

HYPERACTIVITYPOGRAPHER

*You are permitted to use the professional designation
H.A.T. following your name.*

*Signed by an official representative of the
Institute of Hyperactivitypography*

*Signed by a fellow hyperactivitypographer
in awe of your magnificent talent*